The "Karma" Puzzle

Dr.A.K.Saxena, Ph.D.

Published by Dr.A.K.Saxena, Ph.D., 2024.

While every precaution has been taken in the preparation of this book, the publisher assumes no responsibility for errors or omissions, or for damages resulting from the use of the information contained herein.

THE "KARMA" PUZZLE

First edition. November 3, 2024.

Copyright © 2024 Dr.A.K.Saxena, Ph.D..

ISBN: 979-8227791276

Written by Dr.A.K.Saxena, Ph.D..

TABLE OF CONTENTS

1. Introduction

2. *"Karma"*: Definition, History, and Philosophy

3. *"Karma"* in diverse cultures and spiritual traditions

4. The Threefold Law: Cause, Effect, and Consequence

5. *"Karma"* and the Universe: Cosmic Principles and Patterns

6. The Role of Free Will and Personal Responsibility

7. Types of *"Karma"*: *Sanchita, Prarabdha,* and *Kriyamana*

8. *"Karma"* and Reincarnation: The Cycle of Birth and Death

9. The Law of Attraction and *"Karma"*: Manifesting Reality

10. *"Karma"* and Emotions: The Power of Thought and Intention

11. Practicing *"Karma yoga"*: Selfless Action and Service

12. Cultivating Positive *"Karma"*: Virtues and Values

13. Overcoming Negative *"Karma"*: Forgiveness and Release

14. *"Karma"* and Relationships: Interconnectedness and Responsibility

15. *"Karma"* and Spiritual Evolution: Soul Growth and Transformation

16. The Role of Mindfulness and Meditation in *"Karma"*

17. Breaking Free from Karmic Patterns: Liberation and Enlightenment

18. *"Karma"* and the Path to Self-Realization

19. Integrating *"Karma"* into Daily Life: Practical Tips and Strategies

20. The Future of *"Karma"*: Evolving Consciousness and Global Responsibility

21. Conclusion: Embracing the Law of *"Karma"*

22. Glossary of *"Karma"*-related Terms

23. Recommended Reading and Resources

24. Reflection Questions and Exercises

@@@@

CHAPTER 1
INTRODUCTION

"The habits you cultivated in past lives have created your physical, mental, and emotional makeup in this life. You have forgotten those habits, but they have not forgotten you. Out of the crowded centuries of your experiences, your "Karma" follows you. And whenever you are reborn, that "Karma", consisting of all your past thoughts and actions and habits, creates the kind of physical form you will have—not only your appearance, but your personality traits. It is these individually created past-life patterns that make one person different from another, and account for the vast variety of human faces and characteristics. The very fact that you are a woman, or a man was determined by your self-chosen tendencies in previous lives."

Paramhansa Yogananda

"The "Karma" Puzzle": Understanding the Law of Cosmic Justice" is a profound exploration of the ancient and universal principle of *"Karma"*, a concept that has captivated human imagination for centuries. This book delves into the intricate web of cause and effect, revealing the underlying mechanisms that govern our lives and shape our destinies.

For millennia, philosophers, spiritual leaders, and wisdom seekers have grappled with the enigma of *"Karma"*. From the sacred texts of Hinduism and Buddhism to the philosophical musings of ancient Greece and modern thought leaders, the concept of *"Karma"* has evolved, yet its essence remains unchanged: every action, thought, and intention has consequences that reverberate throughout the cosmos.

As we navigate the complexities of life, we often find ourselves pondering fundamental questions:

Why do good things happen to bad people?

Why do we suffer despite our best intentions?

How can we break free from patterns of pain and stagnation?

The *"Karma"* offers answers, providing a comprehensive framework for understanding the cosmic justice that governs our existence.

This book is not merely a theoretical exploration but a practical guide for living in harmony with the karmic principles that govern our universe. Join me on this transformative journey as we unravel the mysteries of the *"Karma"*.

"The "Karma" Puzzle" is more than a book – it's a key to unlocking the secrets of the universe and your place within it. As we embark on this exploration, may the ancient wisdom of *"Karma"* illuminate our path, guiding us toward a life of purpose, balance, and harmony.

@@@@

CHAPTER 2

"KARMA": DEFINITION, HISTORY AND PHILOSOPHY

The concept of *"Karma"* is the one that has been acknowledged and discussed for many centuries in various cultures and religions around the world. It is a concept that has been widely misunderstood and often used in popular culture without a full understanding of its true meaning. In this chapter, we will investigate the definition, history, and philosophy of *"Karma"* to gain a better understanding of its significance and role in our lives.

Definition of "*Karma*"

"Kr" is a Sanskrit term that translates to "action" or "deed." It is a fundamental concept in *Hinduism, Buddhism, Jainism,* and *Sikhism*, where it is believed to be *a fundamental force that governs the universe. "Karma" can be defined as the law of cause and effect, where every action we take has a corresponding reaction or consequence.* This concept is also referred to as the law of moral causation or the law of moral consequences.

According to this belief, every thought, every word, and every action we engage in, creates an imprint or energy that will eventually come back to us in some form. Simply put, this means that if we do good deeds, we will receive positive outcomes, and if we choose to do bad deeds, we will experience negative consequences. To summarise, we can say that *our actions have consequences, whether good or bad.*

"*Karma*" *is often understood as a moralistic, cosmic accounting system, where good deeds and intentions lead to beneficial outcomes, while harmful or malevolent actions result in suffering.*

History of *"Karma"*

The concept of *"Karma"* has its roots in ancient India and has been mentioned in ancient Hindu scriptures such as the *Vedas,* the *Upanishads and the Shrimad Bhagavad Gita.* The concept of karma originated in Vedic period (*1500 BCE - 500 BCE*). The word "karma" is derived from the Sanskrit root "*kr*," meaning "to do" or "to act." Initially, *"karma"* referred to the ritualistic actions and sacrifices performed to maintain cosmic order and ensure individual well-being.

Over time, *"Karma"* evolved to encompass moral and ethical dimensions. The *Upanishads (800 BCE - 400 BCE)* introduced the idea of rebirth and the transmigration of souls, linking *"Karma"* to the cycle of birth, death, and rebirth (*samsara*). The *Bhagavad Gita* (400 BCE) further developed the concept, emphasizing the importance of selfless action (n*ishkama karma*) and the attainment of liberation (*moksha*) through detachment from worldly desires.

Buddhism, emerging in the 6th century BCE, adapted and refined the concept of *"karma"*. The Buddha taught that *"karma"* is not just about actions, but also intentions and mental states. He emphasized the importance of mindfulness, ethics, and compassion in shaping individual *"Karma"*.

In *Hinduism*, "*Karma*" is believed to have originated from *"Brahma"*, the Hindu deity who is believed to have created the universe and set the laws of cause and effect in motion. It is also mentioned in early Buddhist texts as an essential part of the teachings of *Gautama Buddha.*

The concept of "Karma" was introduced to Western society by Swami Vivekananda in the late 19th century. It gained more popularity in the 20th century with the rise of Eastern spirituality and the spread of Hinduism and Buddhism in the West. Today, *"Karma"* is a well-known concept that is widely accepted and discussed in many cultures and religions around the world.

Philosophy of "Karma"

The philosophy of "Karma" goes beyond the simple cause and effect principle. It is a belief that our actions not only have consequences in this life but also in future lives. This is based on the concept of rebirth or reincarnation, where it is believed that our souls are reborn into new bodies after death. In this cycle of birth, death, and rebirth, our "Karma" determines the type of life we will have in the next birth.

According to this philosophy, our current life is a result of our actions in past lives, and our actions in this life will determine our future lives. This creates a sense of responsibility for our actions and encourages us to make positive choices to improve our future lives.

"Karma" also teaches us the importance of living in harmony with nature and others. As we are all interconnected, every action we take has an impact on those around us and the environment. Therefore, it is essential to be mindful of our thoughts, words, and actions to create positive energy and avoid negative consequences.

"Karma" also emphasizes the idea of personal responsibility for one's life. Our circumstances are not solely determined by external factors but also by our own actions. This means that we have the power to change our lives by making positive choices and taking responsibility for our actions.

In *Hinduism*, there are three types of *"Karma"* are believed to exist *viz. Sanchita* (accumulated), *Prarabdha* (fructifying), and *Agami* (future). "*Sanchita Karma*" refers to all the accumulated karmic imprints from our past lives. "*Prarabdha Karma*" is the portion of "*Sanchita Karma*" that has ripened and is currently manifesting in this life. "*Agami Karma*" is the current actions that will determine our future lives.

In Buddhism, the concept of *"Karma"* is closely related to the idea of impermanence and the *Four Noble Truths*. "*Karma*" is seen as a chain of causation that perpetuates suffering, and to break this cycle, one must follow the *Eightfold Path to enlightenment.*

"Karma" in Modern Society

Today, the concept of *"Karma"* is often misunderstood and misused. It is sometimes used to justify the suffering of others or to avoid taking responsibility for one's actions. *However, the true essence of "Karma" lies in its message of personal responsibility and creating positive actions.*

In recent years, there has been an increasing interest in the concept of *"instant Karma"* where people believe that good things will happen to them immediately after doing a good deed. *While this may be true in some cases, it goes against the fundamental principle of "Karma", which envisages that actions have the consequences that may not be immediately visible or experienced.*

Moreover, the concept of *"Karma"* has also been commercialized and used as a marketing tool. Many products and services are marketed as *"Karma"*-friendly" or "good *"Karma"* without truly understanding the depth and complexity of this concept. This commercialization takes away from the true essence and significance of *"Karma".*

Some Key Concepts

1. *Dharma*: Righteous living and adherence to moral principles.

2. *Moksha:* Liberation from the cycle of rebirth and karma.

3. *Nishkama Karma*: Selfless action, performed without attachment to outcomes.

4. *Ahimsa:* Non-harming and compassion towards all living beings.

Criticisms and Controversies

1. **Determinism:** *"Karma"* can be seen as deterministic, implying that individual choices are predetermined.

2. **Fatalism:** *"Karma"* can lead to fatalism, discouraging effort and personal responsibility.

3. **Injustice:** *"Karma"* can be perceived as unjust, as individuals may suffer due to circumstances beyond their control.

Influence and Relevance

"Karma" has influenced various aspects of Eastern culture, including:

1. **Ethics and Morality:** Shaping moral principles and guiding individual behaviour.

2. **Spirituality and Religion:** Informing concepts of rebirth, liberation, and enlightenment.

3. **Psychology and Philosophy:** Inspiring reflection on personal responsibility, free will, and the nature of reality.

4. **Social Justice:** Encouraging compassion, empathy, and social responsibility.

In conclusion, *"karma"* is a complex and multifaceted concept that has evolved over thousands of years. Its rich history, philosophy, and principles continue to shape Eastern spirituality, ethics, and culture, offering insights into the nature of reality, personal responsibility, and the human condition.

@@@@

CHAPTER 3

UNDERSTANDING "KARMA" IN DIFFERENT CULTURES AND TRADITION

"Karma" is a fundamental concept in various cultures and spiritual traditions around the world. *It is a belief that the actions and intentions of an individual in one life will have an impact on their future lives and experiences. This idea of cause and effect has been interpreted differently in different cultures, but the underlying principle remains the same – that our actions have consequences.*

The Origins of *"Karma"*

The concept of *"Karma"* can be traced back to ancient Indian religions such as Hinduism, Buddhism, and Jainism. In these religions, *"Karma"* is seen as a spiritual law that governs the cycle of birth, death, and rebirth. It is believed that every action, good or bad, creates an imprint on a person's soul or consciousness, which will determine their destiny in future lives. This cycle continues until a person attains enlightenment and breaks free from the cycle of rebirth.

In Hinduism, *"Karma"* is closely linked to the concept of dharma, which means fulfilling one's duty and moral obligations. It is believed that by following dharma, one can accumulate positive *"Karma"* and improve their chances of a better life in their next incarnation.

Buddhism also has a strong belief in *"Karma"* but approaches it from a slightly different perspective. In Buddhism, the goal is to end suffering and achieve enlightenment. The concept of *"Karma"* is seen to understand how our actions can lead to suffering or happiness in this life and the next. Buddha taught that by following the Eightfold Path, one can break free from the cycle of rebirth and attain *nirvana*.

"Karma" in Other Eastern Religions

The concept of "Karma" is not limited to Indian religions; it can also be found in other Eastern traditions such as Taoism and Confucianism. In Taoism, *"Karma"* is referred to as *"dao"* or the way. It is believed that by following the natural flow of life and living in harmony with the universe, one can avoid negative *"Karma"* and achieve balance and peace.

In Confucianism, *"Karma"* is known as *"li,"* which translates to "ritual propriety" or "propriety." It is seen as a moral that one must follow to maintain a harmonious relationship with society and the universe. By practicing li, one can accumulate positive *"Karma"* and attain a better life in the future.

"Karma" in Western Religions

While the concept of *"Karma"* originated in Eastern religions, it has also found its way into Western belief systems. In *Judaism*, for instance, the concept of *"Karma"* is referred to as *"middah k'neged middah,"* which means *"measure for measure."* It is believed that one's actions will be rewarded or punished in this life, or the afterlife based on their deeds.

In *Christianity*, the concept of *"Karma"* is not explicitly mentioned, but the idea of sowing and reaping can be seen as similar. The *Bible* states, *"Whatever a man sows, that he will also reap."* This means that our actions have consequences, and we will face the repercussions of our choices in this life or the next.

"Karma" in Modern Society

In today's modern society, the concept of *"Karma"* has been adopted by many to understand and navigate their lives. It has become a popular belief that what goes around comes around – that our actions will have consequences, whether positive or negative. This idea has been embraced by many individuals, including those who do not follow a specific religious tradition.

The Law of Attraction, popularized by the book and film *"The Secret,"* is also based on the concept of *"Karma"*. It suggests that by focusing on positive thoughts and intentions, one can attract positive outcomes in their life. Similarly, the practice of mindfulness, which encourages individuals to be aware of their thoughts and actions, is also rooted in the concept of *"Karma"*.

"Karma" in Action

The idea of *"Karma"* can be seen in action in various ways, both on an individual and societal level. On an individual level, someone who is kind and compassionate towards others is likely to receive kindness and compassion in return. On the other hand, someone who harms others will face negative consequences for their actions.

On a societal level, the concept of *"Karma"* can be seen in the form of societal norms and laws. These are based on the idea that certain actions are considered right or wrong, and those who follow these norms will be rewarded while those who break them will face punishment.

Ancient Greece and Western Philosophy

Western philosophers like *Plato* and *Aristotle* touched on *"Karma"*-like concepts:

1. **The Law of Retribution:** Wrongdoers face punishment.

2. **The Concept of Nemesis:** Excessive pride invites divine retribution.

Indigenous Cultures: Balance and Reciprocity

Many indigenous cultures believe in *"Karma"*-like principles:

1. **Native American:** The *Great Law of the Iroquois* emphasizes balance and reciprocity.

2. **African:** Ancestors' actions influence descendants' lives.

Modern Interpretations

Contemporary thinkers have adapted *"Karma"* to suit modern contexts:

1. **New Age Spirituality:** *"Karma"* as personal responsibility and manifestation.

2. **Psychological Karma:** Unconscious patterns and emotional baggage.

Common Threads

Despite cultural variations, *"Karma"* shares common themes:

1. **Cause-and-Effect:** Actions have consequences.

2. **Moral Responsibility:** Individuals are accountable for their choices.

3. **Spiritual Growth:** *"Karma"* facilitates self-improvement and liberation.

Karma's diverse interpretations across cultures and traditions demonstrate its timeless relevance. Embracing *Karma's* principles encourages mindfulness, compassion, and personal growth, leading to a more harmonious and balanced existence.

@@@@

CHAPTER 4

<u>THE THREEFOLD LAW: CAUSE, EFFECT AND CONSEQUENCE</u>

"Karma" is a widely known and talked about concept in the spiritual community. It is often referred to as the law of cause and effect and is believed to play a major role in shaping our lives. The term *"Karma"* comes from the Sanskrit word *"kr"* meaning "action" or "deed." In simple terms, it means that our actions have consequences. However, *the concept of "Karma" goes beyond just action and consequence. It is a complex and multi-faceted concept that encompasses the threefold law of cause, effect, and consequence.*

The Threefold Law of *"Karma"* is rooted in the belief that every action we take has a ripple effect on our lives. It is believed that every thought, word, and action we put out into the universe creates an energy that will eventually come back to us in some form. This law is often explained through the analogy of sowing and reaping – just like a farmer who sows seeds and reaps a harvest, so too do our actions result in consequences.

The First Fold: Cause (*"Karma"*)

The first fold, cause, refers to the initial action, thought, or intention that sets the karmic process in motion. This cause can be:

1. **Volitional:** Conscious choices and decisions.

2. **Non-Volitional:** Unconscious patterns or habitual actions.

3. **Intentional:** Actions driven by purpose and motivation.

This refers to the actions, thoughts, and intentions that we put out into the world. Every action we take, whether it is positive or negative, has an impact on our surroundings. For example, if we choose to help someone in need, our action will have a positive impact not only on that person but also on those around us. On the other hand, if we choose to harm someone or act selfishly, it will create negative energy not only for others but also for ourselves. This is why it is important to be mindful of our thoughts and actions because they have the power to create the 'cause' which will eventually lead to an 'effect.' Every cause has a specific energy signature, influencing the subsequent effect.

The Second Fold: Effect (*Kriya*)

The effect, or *kriya*, is the immediate result of the cause. This can manifest as:

1. **Immediate Consequences**: Direct outcomes of the action.

2. **Latent Tendencies**: Seeds planted for future consequences.

3. **Energy Imprints**: Residual energies influencing future experiences.

This refers to the consequences of our actions. The energy we put out into the universe will come back to us, either in this lifetime or in future lifetimes. *This can manifest in various forms such as experiences, events, relationships, and even our physical and mental well-being.* For instance, if we consistently put out positive energy through our actions, we are more likely to attract positive experiences and relationships into our lives. On the other hand, if we constantly engage in negative actions, we may experience negative consequences such as conflicts, setbacks, and challenges.

It is important to note that the 'effect' of our actions is not always immediate. Just like a seed takes time to grow into a plant, the effects of our actions may take time to manifest. This is why we may sometimes see people experiencing sudden success or failure without any apparent cause – it could be a result of their past actions coming to fruition.

The effect amplifies or diminishes the original energy, depending on the nature of the cause.

The Third Fold: Consequence (*Karmaphala*)

The consequence, or *karmaphala*, is the ultimate outcome of the karmic process. This can manifest as:

1. **Short-Term Consequences:** Immediate rewards or repercussions.

2. **Long-Term Consequences:** Future experiences shaped by past actions.

3. **Cumulative Consequences:** Accumulated *"Karma"* from multiple causes.

Consequences can be:

1. **Sanchita:** Accumulated *"Karma"* from past lives.

2. **Kriyamana:** Current life's *"Karma"*.

3. **Agami:** Future *"Karma"*, shaped by present choices.

The final part of the threefold law is 'consequence.'

This refers to the ultimate result of our actions – good or bad. Our actions create a ripple effect that not only affects us but also those around us. In this sense, we are all interconnected and responsible for each other's well-being. The concept of *'what goes around comes around'* reflects this law of *"Karma"* – our actions will eventually come back to us in some form.

Interplay Between the Three Folds

The threefold law demonstrates a dynamic interplay:

1. **Cause-and-Effect:** Each cause generates an effect.

2. **Effect-Consequence:** The effect ripens into consequence.

3. **Consequence-Cause:** Consequences influence future causes.

Key Principles

1. **Asylum:** Every action has an equal and opposite reaction.

2. **Non-Randomness:** Karma is not arbitrary; effects are directly tied to causes.

3. **Moral Responsibility:** Individuals are accountable for their actions.

4. **Causality:** Causes precede effects.

Implications and Applications

1. **Personal Growth:** Recognize patterns, break free from negative cycles.

2. **Mindfulness:** Intentional actions, thoughtful decisions.

3. **Compassion:** Empathy for self and others, understanding karmic struggles.

4. **Forgiveness:** Release negative energies, liberate from karmic burdens.

Practical Strategies

1. **Self-Reflection:** Examine motivations, actions, and consequences.

2. **Mindful Decision-Making:** Consider potential consequences.

3. **Karmic Cleansing:** Release negative patterns, energies.

4. **Spiritual Practices:** Cultivate compassion, wisdom, and inner peace.

The threefold law of *"Karma"* offers a nuanced understanding of the intricate web of cause, effect, and consequence. By grasping this fundamental principle, individuals can:

1. **Take Responsibility**: Acknowledge agency in shaping destiny.
2. **Make Informed Choices:** Consider potential consequences.
3. **Cultivate Mindfulness:** Align actions with values and compassion.

Embracing the threefold law empowers us to navigate life's complexities with awareness, wisdom, and karmic intelligence.

It is, however, important to understand that the threefold law of "Karma" is not a punishment or reward system. It simply states that our actions have consequences and encourages us to take responsibility for our choices. We cannot control all the events and circumstances in our lives, but we can control how we respond to them. This is where the concept of free will comes into play – we have the power to choose our thoughts and actions, which in turn will shape our lives.

Now, one may question why we may experience challenges or difficulties even when we have always put out positive energy into the universe. This brings us to another important aspect of *"Karma"* – the concept of past lives. It is believed that our actions and experiences in past lives also have an impact on our current life. This means that we may be facing challenges or rewards based on our actions in past lives, which we may not necessarily remember.

The concept of "Karma" can be seen as a spiritual guide that encourages us to be mindful of our actions and thoughts. It teaches us to take responsibility for our choices and reminds us that we have the power to create our own reality. It also reminds us to practice empathy and compassion towards others, as our actions not only affect ourselves but also those around us.

In conclusion, the threefold law of *"Karma"* – cause, effect, and consequence – is a complex yet profound concept that helps us understand the role of our actions in shaping our lives. It reminds us to be mindful of our thoughts and actions, as they have the power to create a ripple effect that will eventually come back to us. By understanding and embracing this law, we can strive towards creating positive energy and experiences in our lives and the world around us. As the famous saying goes, *"The best way to predict your future is to create it."* Let us use the power of "Karma" to create a bright and positive future for ourselves and others.

@@@@

CHAPTER 5

"KARMA" AND THE UNIVERSE: COSMIC PRINCIPLES AND PATTERNS

The concept of *"Karma"* and the universe has been a topic of interest and discussion for centuries. It has been explored and interpreted by various religions, spiritual traditions, and philosophies. However, it is still a complex and elusive concept for many. In this chapter, we will look into the depths of *"Karma"* and the universe, exploring its cosmic principles and patterns.

"Kr" is a Sanskrit word that means "action" or "deed." In its simplest form, it refers to the law of cause and effect, where our actions have consequences. The idea of *"Karma"* suggests that our thoughts, words, and actions create an energetic force that will eventually come back to us in some form or another.

According to the Hindu belief, *"Karma"* is an integral part of our existence, and it is governed by the laws of the universe. These laws dictate that every action we take, whether positive or negative, will have a corresponding effect on our future. This means that our present circumstances are a result of our past actions, and our future will be shaped by our present actions.

The concept of *"Karma"* can also be found in other religions like Buddhism, Jainism, Sikhism, and Taoism. In Buddhism, *"Karma"* is seen as a natural law of the universe that works alongside other universal laws such as impermanence and interdependence. In Jainism, *"Karma"* is viewed as a physical substance that attaches to the soul and determines its future experiences.

While *"Karma"* is commonly associated with reincarnation and rebirth in Eastern religions, it also holds significance in Western religions like

Christianity. The biblical principle of *"you reap what you sow"* can be seen as a reflection of the concept of *"Karma"*.

The universe, on the other hand, refers to all matter, energy, time, and space that exist in the vast expanse beyond Earth. It encompasses everything we can see and cannot see, including galaxies, stars, planets, and all living beings. The universe is a complex and intricate system that is constantly expanding and evolving.

The relationship between *"Karma"* and the universe can be understood through the idea of interconnectedness. Everything in the universe is connected, and our actions have a ripple effect that can impact the entire cosmos. Just like a pebble thrown into a pond creates ripples, our thoughts, words, and actions create vibrations that can have far-reaching consequences.

Cosmic Principles

1. The Law of Cause and Effect:

Every action, thought, and intention has consequences, echoing throughout the universe.

2. The Principle of Resonance:

Energies vibrational frequency attracts similar energies, influencing *"Karma"*

3. The Law of Attraction:

Like attracts like; thoughts and intentions draw corresponding experiences.

4. The Principle of Balance:

The universe seeks equilibrium; *"Karma"* restores balance.

One of the cosmic principles of *"Karma"* and the universe is balance.

The universe seeks to maintain balance and harmony, and *"Karma"* plays a crucial role in achieving this. Our actions, whether positive or negative, have a boomerang effect that will eventually return to us. This is why it is essential to be mindful of our thoughts and actions, as they can have a significant impact on our present and future.

Another cosmic principle of *"Karma"* and the universe is impermanence.

The universe is in a constant state of flux, and nothing remains the same forever. This applies to our actions as well – what goes around comes around. Our good deeds may not bring immediate rewards, but they will eventually manifest in some form or another.

The concept of *"Karma"* also involves the idea of free will.

While we may be subject to the consequences of our past actions, we also have the power to create our future through our present actions. Our thoughts, words, and actions are like seeds that we plant in the garden of life. We have the freedom to choose which seeds we want to nurture and grow.

Furthermore, *"Karma"* teaches us about responsibility.

We are responsible for our own actions and their consequences. It prompts us to take ownership of our lives and make conscious choices that align with our values. We cannot control what happens to us, but we can control how we respond to it.

***"Karma"* also highlights the concept of interconnectedness between all living beings.**

Our actions not only affect us but also those around us. This understanding can help us cultivate empathy and compassion towards others, as we realize the impact of our actions on their lives.

"Karma" and the Universe: Unveiling Cosmic Principles and Patterns

The concept of *"Karma"*, often associated with individual actions and consequences, extends far beyond personal experiences, resonating with the fundamental principles governing the universe. This article explores the intricate relationships between *"Karma"*, cosmic laws, and universal patterns, revealing the profound harmony between human existence and the celestial landscape.

Universal Patterns

1. Cycles of Time: *"Karma"* unfolds through cycles of birth, growth, decay, and renewal.

2. Spiral Dynamics: *"Karma"* evolves through spiral patterns, reflecting growth and transformation.

3. Fractals and Self-Similarity: *"Karma"* replicates patterns across scales, from personal to cosmic.

Karmic Connections to Celestial Bodies

1. Planetary Influences: Planets and stars imbue energies, shaping individual *"Karma"*.

2. Astral Cycles: Celestial events (eclipses, planetary alignments) impact collective *"Karma"*.

3. Cosmic Rhythms: Galactic cycles and universal vibrations guide karmic unfoldment.

Karmic Reflections in Nature

The patterns of *"Karma"* can also be seen in the cycles and rhythms of nature. Just like the changing of seasons, our lives go through cycles of growth, decay, and rebirth. The universe teaches us that everything is temporary, and we must learn to let go and embrace change. The patterns of *"Karma"* in rhythms of nature could be:

1. **Seasonal Cycles:** Growth, decay, and renewal mirror karmic patterns.

2. **Ecosystems:** Interconnectedness and balance demonstrate *"Karma'*s principle.

3. **Natural Laws:** Gravity, electromagnetism, and thermodynamics illustrate *"Karma'*s operation.

Quantum *"Karma"*

1. **Entanglement:** Connectedness across space and time reflects *"Karma'*s non-locality.

2. **Wave-Particle Duality:** *"Karma'*s dual nature (cause-effect, intention-consequence).

3. **Uncertainty Principle:** *Karma's* unpredictability and the role of observation.

Consciousness and Karma

1. **Collective Unconscious:** Shared *"Karma"* and archetypes.

2. **Personal Consciousness:** Individual *"Karma"* and self-awareness.

3. **Cosmic Consciousness:** Universal awareness and interconnectedness.

Implications and Applications

1. **Holistic Understanding:** Recognize *"Karma's* universal context.

2. **Cosmic Responsibility:** Acknowledge agency in shaping reality.

3. **Harmonious Living:** Align actions with cosmic principles.

"Karma" and the universe are intertwined, reflecting a profound harmony between human existence and celestial dynamics. Embracing cosmic principles and patterns empowers us to:

1. **Understand *Karma's* universal context.**

2. **Align with celestial rhythms.**

3. **Cultivate harmony and balance.**

By recognizing *"Karma's* intricate relationships with the universe, we may navigate life's complexities with wisdom, compassion, and cosmic awareness.

Moreover, the concept of *"Karma"* and the universe invites us to look beyond ourselves and think about the greater good. It prompts us to consider the consequences of our actions on a global scale and encourages us to act in ways that benefit not just ourselves but also others and the planet.

In conclusion, *"Karma"* and the universe are intertwined cosmic principles that govern our existence. They teach us about balance, impermanence, interconnectedness, responsibility, and free will. Understanding these concepts can help us live a more conscious and intentional life, where we take ownership of our actions and strive to create a positive impact on ourselves and the world around us. As we continue to navigate this complex and ever-evolving universe, let us remember the wise words of *Mahatma Gandhi* – *"The future depends on what you do today."* So let us practice good "Karma" in our present to create a better future for ourselves and the universe.

@@@@

CHAPTER 6

<u>THE ROLE OF FREE WILL AND PERSONAL RESPONSIBILITY</u>

In life, we are constantly faced with choices and decisions that shape our actions and ultimately define who we are. These choices may seem small and insignificant, or they may be life-changing, but one thing remains constant – they are our own to make. *This concept of having control over our actions and decisions is known as free will.* At the same time, *we also have the responsibility to take ownership of these actions and their consequences, which is known as personal responsibility.* In this chapter, we will discuss the role of free will and personal responsibility in our lives and why they are crucial for personal growth and development.

Firstly, let us define the terms "free will" and "personal responsibility." Free will can be described as the power or ability to make choices that are not determined by external factors. It is the belief that individuals have control over their actions and can choose their own path in life. On the other hand, personal responsibility refers to the duty and accountability for one's own actions, behaviors, and decisions. It is the understanding that our choices have consequences, and we must take ownership of those consequences.

Now, **why are these concepts so important in our lives?** One of the main reasons is that they give us a sense of agency and control over our lives. It is empowering to know that we have the freedom to make our own choices and that our actions have an impact. This sense of agency also allows us to take charge of our lives and work towards achieving our goals and aspirations.

Moreover, *free will and personal responsibility go hand in hand. Our ability to make choices freely also comes with the responsibility to take ownership of those choices.* We cannot claim to have free will if we do not accept personal responsibility for our actions. We must understand that every decision we make has consequences, whether positive or negative, and it is up to us to face those consequences.

Another crucial aspect of free will and personal responsibility is their role in personal growth and development. When we have the freedom to make our own choices, we also can learn from our mistakes. Taking responsibility for our actions allows us to reflect on our decisions and understand where we may have gone wrong. This self-reflection is crucial for personal growth as it helps us make better choices in the future. It also allows us to take accountability for our actions and make amends if necessary.

Furthermore, **free will and personal responsibility also play a significant role in our relationships with others.** When we acknowledge that we have control over our actions, we also accept that others have the same freedom. This understanding can lead to more compassionate and empathetic relationships as we recognize that everyone is responsible for their own choices and behaviors.

However, it is essential to note that while we have free will, it is not absolute. There are certain external factors that can influence our choices, such as societal norms, cultural beliefs, and upbringing. These factors may limit our free will, but they do not eliminate it entirely. It is still up to us to make conscious decisions and take responsibility for them.

Moreover, some may argue that free will does not exist, as everything is predetermined. This belief is known as determinism, which suggests that all events, including human actions, are determined by previous events or natural laws. While this debate has been ongoing for centuries, it is essential to remember that whether free will exists or not, the concept of personal responsibility remains unchanged. We must still take ownership of our actions and their consequences.

The Interplay of Free Will and Personal Responsibility in Karma and the Universe

The concepts of free will and personal responsibility are intricately woven into the fabric of *"Karma"*, influencing the unfolding of individual and collective destinies. This article explores the dynamic relationship between free will, personal responsibility, and *"Karma"*, shedding light on the complexities of cosmic justice and human agency.

Free Will: The Power of Choice

Free will is the capacity to make choices, unhindered by external coercion or determinism. In the context of karma:

1. **Volitional Actions:** Conscious decisions shape *"Karma"*.

2. **Intentional Choices:** Motivations and intentions influence karmic outcomes.

3. **Moral Agency:** Individuals are accountable for their actions.

Personal Responsibility: Embracing Consequences

Personal responsibility acknowledges the consequences of choices, recognizing:

1. **Causal Connection:** Actions have effects.

2. **Moral Causality:** Choices impact karma.

3. **Self-Accountability:** Individuals answer for their decisions.

Karmic Dynamics: Interplay between Free Will and Personal Responsibility

1. **Karmic Accumulation:** Choices accumulate karma.
2. **Karmic Debt:** Unresolved energies manifest as challenges.
3. **Karmic Liberation:** Conscious choices lead to liberation.

Cosmic Context: Universal Principles

1. **Law of Cause and Effect:** Actions have consequences.
2. **Law of Attraction:** Energies attract similar experiences.
3. **Principle of Balance:** Universe seeks equilibrium.

The Role of Intention

Intention plays a crucial role in karmic dynamics:

1. **Motivation:** Intentions behind actions influence karma.
2. **Consciousness:** Awareness of intentions shapes karmic outcomes.
3. **Alignment:** Intentions aligned with universal principles facilitate growth.

Navigating Free Will and Personal Responsibility

1. **Self-Awareness:** Recognize thoughts, emotions, and intentions.
2. **Mindful Decision-Making:** Consider consequences.
3. **Embracing Responsibility:** Acknowledge and learn from mistakes.

Challenges and Limitations

1. **Conditioning and Programming:** Environmental and societal influences.

2. **Unconscious Patterns:** Hidden biases and habits.

3. **Karmic Conditioning:** Past experiences shape present choices.

Spiritual Perspectives

1. **Hinduism:** Free will (*Purushartha*) and *"Karma"*.

2. **Buddhism:** Intention (*Chetanā*) and karmic consequences.

3. *Taoism:* Harmony with the *Tao*, balancing free will and destiny.

Practical Applications

1. **Mindfulness and Meditation:** Cultivate awareness.

2. **Self-Reflection and Journaling:** Examine intentions and choices.

3. **Seeking Guidance:** Consult spiritual teachers or mentors.

The interplay between free will and personal responsibility is central to understanding *"Karma"* and the universe. *Embracing this dynamic empowers individuals to:*

1. **Make conscious choices.**

2. **Acknowledge consequences.**

3. **Cultivate self-awareness and responsibility.**

By recognizing the significance of free will and personal responsibility, we may navigate life's complexities with wisdom, compassion, and karmic intelligence.

In conclusion, the concepts of free will and personal responsibility are vital for leading a fulfilling and purposeful life. They give us a sense of control over our lives and allow us to take charge of our decisions. They also play a significant role in personal growth and development, as well as in maintaining healthy relationships with others. So, the next time you are faced with a decision, remember that you have the freedom to choose and the responsibility to take ownership of that choice.

@@@

CHAPTER 7

TYPES OF *"KARMA"*: *"SANCHITA"*, *"PRARABDHA"* AND *"KRIYAMANA"*

"Karma" is a concept that is deeply ingrained in many spiritual and religious traditions. It is often defined as the sum of a person's actions in this and previous states of existence, viewed as deciding their fate in future existences. In simpler terms, it refers to the law of cause and effect, where our actions have consequences that affect our present and future. However, *"Karma"* can be further broken down into different types based on its nature and impact. In this chapter, we will look deeper into the three types of *"Karma"*: *"Sanchit"*, *"Prarabdha"*, and *"Kriyamana."*

"Sanchit Karma":

"Sanchit Karma" can be translated as *"accumulated Karma" or "stored Karma"*. It refers to the sum of all our past actions and their consequences, both good and bad, that have not yet manifested. *Think of it as a bank account where we deposit all our actions and intentions throughout our lifetimes. These actions can be from our current lifetime or past lifetimes.*

Sanchit *"Karma"* is not limited to just one lifetime; it carries over from one lifetime to another until it is exhausted. *This explains why some people may experience certain events or circumstances that seem unexplainable based on their current actions.* It is believed that our "Sanchit *Karma*" plays a significant role in determining the circumstances of our birth, including our family, social status, and physical and mental abilities.

However, *"Sanchit Karma"* can be modified or reduced through spiritual practices such as meditation, *yoga*, and selfless service *(seva)*.

These practices help us become more aware of our actions and intentions, leading to better decision-making and affecting our future *"Sanchit Karma"*.

"Prarabdha Karma":

"Prarabdha Karma" can be translated as *"ripe or fructified Karma"* or *"destined Karma"*. It is a subset of *"Sanchit Karma"* and refers to the portion of our accumulated *"Karma"* that is ripe and ready to manifest in our current lifetime. In simple terms, it is the *"Karma"* that we are currently experiencing and that we cannot avoid or change.

Our *"Prarabdha Karma"* determines the circumstances of our current life, including our physical and mental health, relationships, and career. *It is seen as the "destiny" that we are born with, and it cannot be altered. This does not mean that we are completely helpless in the face of our "Prarabdha Karma". Our response to these circumstances can create new "Sanchit Karma", which can then modify our future "Prarabdha Karma".*

For example, if someone is born into a wealthy family due to their *"Sanchit Karma"*, their *"Prarabdha Karma"* may manifest as health issues or challenges in their relationships. However, they may choose to respond to these challenges positively by practicing gratitude and compassion, leading to a more positive *"Sanchit Karma"* in the future.

"Kriyamana Karma":

"Kriyamana Karma" can be translated as "current or immediate Karma" or "action-based "Karma". *It refers to the actions we are currently performing and their consequences. Unlike "sanchit" and "prarabdha Karma", "Kriyamana Karma" is not predetermined; it is created in the present moment through our free will and choices.*

Our thoughts, words, and deeds all contribute to our *"Kriyamana Karma"*. Every action we take has a ripple effect on our present and future. This type of *"Karma"* teaches us that we are responsible for our actions and must be mindful of our intentions.

"Kriyamana Karma" can be compared to a seed that we plant today and will eventually grow into a tree with its own set of consequences. Therefore, *it is essential to cultivate positive intentions and actions in the present moment to create a better future for us.*

The Importance of Understanding the Types of "*Karma*":

Understanding the different types of *"Karma"* can help us make sense of our experiences and the world around us. It teaches us that our actions have consequences and that we are responsible for our own fate. By understanding the nature of *"Karma"*, we can become more mindful of our thoughts, words, and deeds, leading to a more conscious and intentional way of living.

Moreover, understanding *"Sanchit"*, *"Prarabdha"*, and *"Kriyamana Karma"* can help us break free from the cycle of suffering. By becoming aware of our accumulated *"Karma"* (*Sanchit*), we can modify it through our actions in the present (*Kriyamana*) and change our destiny (*Prarabdha*) for the better.

@@@@

CHAPTER 8

"KARMA" AND REINCARNATION: THE CYCLE OF BIRTH AND DEATH

"Karma" and reincarnation are two interconnected concepts that have been a part of many ancient and contemporary spiritual beliefs and philosophies. They have gained popularity in recent times due to the increasing interest in Eastern spiritual practices such as Buddhism, Hinduism, and Jainism. *These concepts explain the cyclical nature of life and death, and how our actions in this life can affect our future existence.*

To truly understand the concept of *"Karma"* and reincarnation, we must look into their origins and meanings. *"Karma"* is derived from the Sanskrit word *"kr"* meaning action or deed. It refers to the principle that every action we take has a consequence, whether positive or negative. In other words, what goes around comes around. This idea can be found in many religions, including *Hinduism, Jainism,* and *Buddhism.*

On the other hand, *reincarnation, also known as rebirth, is the belief that after death, the soul or consciousness of an individual is reborn into another physical body. This cycle is believed to continue until one reaches a state of enlightenment or liberation from the cycle of birth and death.* Reincarnation is closely related to the law of *"Karma"* as it suggests that our actions in this life will determine our future existence.

"Karma" and Reincarnation: Unveiling the Cycle of Birth and Death

Reincarnation, a fundamental concept in Eastern spirituality, is deeply intertwined with the principle of *"Karma"*. This cycle of birth, death, and rebirth is believed to be governed by the universal law of cause and effect, where an individual's actions in past lives influence their present and future existences.

Understanding Reincarnation

1. **Cycle of Birth, Death, and Rebirth:** Reincarnation is the cycle of birth, death, and rebirth, where the soul journeys through multiple lives.

2. **Opportunity for Growth:** Reincarnation provides opportunities for growth, learning, and spiritual evolution.

3. **Soul's Journey:** The soul's journey through multiple lives is guided by *"Karma"*.

The Cycle of Birth and Death

1. **Birth:** The soul incarnates, influenced by past *"Karma"*.

2. **Life:** Experiences are shaped by *"Karma"*, choices made, and actions taken.

3. **Death:** *"Karma"* is accumulated, and the soul transitions.

4. **Rebirth:** The cycle repeats, influenced by past *"Karma"*.

Karmic Influences on Reincarnation

1. **"*Sanchita Karma*:"** Accumulated *"Karma"* from past lives influences current life.

2. **"*Kriyamana Karma*":** Current life's actions shape future *"Karma"*.

3. **"*Agami Karma*":** Future *"Karma"* is influenced by present choices.

Types of Reincarnation

1. **Instant Reincarnation**: Immediate rebirth, often seen in cases of sudden death.

2. **Interval Reincarnation**: Period between lives, allowing for reflection and growth.

3. **Spiritual Reincarnation**: Soul's evolution, transcendence, and liberation.

The Role of Free Will and Personal Responsibility

1. **Choices and Actions**: Shape *"Karma"*, influence reincarnation.

2. **Personal Responsibility**: Acknowledge, learn from mistakes.

3. **Free Will**: Exercise conscious choices.

Spiritual Perspectives on *"Karma"* and Reincarnation

1. **Hinduism**: Cycle of birth, death, and rebirth (*samsara*).

2. **Buddhism**: Rebirth driven by *"Karma"*, craving (*"tanha"* meaning thirst, desire, longing, greed*)*.

3. **Jainism**: Soul's journey through multiple lives (*samsarana*).

Breaking the Cycle of Reincarnation

1. **Spiritual Growth**: Transcend *"Karma"*, achieve liberation.

2. **Self-Realization**: Understand true nature.

3. *Moksha*: Attain freedom from rebirth.

Practical Applications

1. **Mindfulness**: Recognize *"Karma"*'s influence.

2. **Self-Reflection**: Analyze actions, intentions.

3. **Spiritual Practices**: Meditation, *yoga*, and self-inquiry.

"Karma" and reincarnation form an intricate web, guiding the soul's journey through multiple lives. *Understanding this cycle empowers individuals to:*

1. **Recognize "Karma's influence.**

2.**Exercise free will and personal responsibility.**

3. **Strive for spiritual growth and liberation.**

Embracing the principles of "Karma" and reincarnation illuminates the path to self-realization, liberation, and ultimate freedom from the cycle of birth and death.

The concept of *"Karma"* and reincarnation has been a subject of debate and fascination for centuries. Some believe in these concepts wholeheartedly, while others dismiss them as mere superstition. However, regardless of one's beliefs, it is essential to understand the significance of these concepts in various spiritual traditions.

In Hinduism, *"Karma"* plays a vital role in shaping one's present and future life. According to Hinduism, every individual is born with a unique karmic account, consisting of the actions from their past lives. This account determines their current life circumstances and challenges. Hindus believe that by fulfilling their duties and living a righteous life, one can improve their *"Karma"* and break the cycle of reincarnation.

Similarly, in Buddhism, *"Karma"* and rebirth are closely linked. The Buddha taught that our actions, thoughts, and intentions create *"Karma"*, which can have an impact on our future lives. The aim of human life in Buddhism is to break the cycle of rebirth by achieving enlightenment through the Eightfold Path.

Jainism also shares a similar belief in *"Karma"* and reincarnation. Jains believe that the quality of one's actions determines the quality of their next birth. The goal in Jainism is to attain *moksha*, liberation from the cycle of birth and death, through self-discipline and spiritual purification.

The concept of *"Karma"* and reincarnation also has practical implications in our daily lives. It encourages individuals to take responsibility for their actions and understand how their choices can impact not only their current life but also their future existence. By living a life guided by positive intentions and actions, one can create a better future for themselves.

Moreover, *this concept also offers solace to those who have lost loved ones. The belief in reincarnation suggests that death is not the end but a mere transition into another life. It provides comfort by offering the possibility of being reunited with loved ones in future lives.*

However, it is essential to understand that the concept of *"Karma"* and reincarnation is not meant to be used as an excuse for suffering or inequality. It does not imply that those who are experiencing hardships in this life are being punished for their actions in past lives. Instead, it teaches us to accept the consequences of our actions and strive towards improving ourselves in this life.

Furthermore, it is crucial to note that *"Karma"* and reincarnation are not limited to only religious beliefs. *There is growing scientific research that suggests the possibility of past lives and the existence of consciousness beyond the physical body. This further supports the idea that our actions in this life can have an impact on our future existence.*

@@@@

CHAPTER 9

THE LAW OF ATTRACTION AND "*KARMA*": MANIFESTING REALITY

The concept of the Law of Attraction and *"Karma"* has gained immense popularity in recent years, especially with the rise of books like *"The Secret"* and movies like *"What the Bleep Do We Know?"* But what exactly are these laws and how do they work together to shape our reality? In this chapter, we will investigate the depths of these universal principles and understand how they play a crucial role in manifesting our desires.

The Law of Attraction states that like attracts like. Simply put, our thoughts and feelings have the power to attract similar experiences, people, and circumstances into our lives. This law is based on the belief that everything in the universe is made up of energy, including our thoughts and emotions. Therefore, what we focus on and give attention to becomes our reality.

But how does this relate to *"Karma"*?

"Karma", a concept derived from ancient Indian traditions, is often misunderstood as a form of punishment for one's actions. However, *it is more accurately described as the law of cause and effect. It states that every action we take has a corresponding consequence or reaction. This can be seen as a balance sheet of our deeds, determining our future experiences.*

So how do these two laws work together?

The Law of Attraction is focused on our thoughts and emotions, while *"Karma"* is focused on our actions. Simply put, our thoughts and emotions attract experiences into our lives, while our actions determine the quality of those experiences.

For example, if we constantly think about being financially stable and successful, but at the same time make poor financial decisions or take no action towards achieving success, we may not see any positive results. This is because our actions do not align with our thoughts and feelings. On the other hand, if we have positive thoughts about abundance and take steps towards achieving financial stability, we may see an increase in wealth as our actions align with our thoughts.

This is where the concept of the manifesting reality comes into play. The law of attraction and "Karma" work together to create our reality. Our thoughts and emotions attract experiences into our lives, and our actions determine the quality of those experiences. Therefore, it is essential to not only have positive thoughts and feelings but also take positive actions towards manifesting our desires.

The Law of Attraction and *"Karma"* are two fundamental principles that shape our reality. Understanding their dynamic relationship empowers us to manifest our desires, overcome challenges, and cultivate spiritual growth.

Manifesting Reality

To manifest reality effectively:

1. **Align Thoughts and Intentions:** Focus on positive, clear desires.

2. **Raise Vibrational Frequency**: Cultivate gratitude, love, and joy.

3. **Recognize Karma**: Acknowledge past actions, thoughts, and intentions.

4. **Make Conscious Choices**: Exercise free will, considering karma.

5. **Let Go of Resistance:** Release negative patterns, emotions.

The Role of Mindfulness

Mindfulness bridges the Law of Attraction and Karma:

1. **Present-Moment Awareness:** Recognize thoughts, emotions.

2. **Intentional Focus**: Concentrate on desires, positivity.

3. **Non-Judgment**: Release attachment to outcomes.

Spiritual Growth

Embracing the Law of Attraction and "Karma" fosters spiritual growth:

1. **Self-Awareness:** Understand thoughts, emotions, intentions.

2. **Personal Responsibility:** Acknowledge karma.

3. **Compassion**: Cultivate empathy, forgiveness.

Practical Applications

Integrate these principles into daily life:

1. **Visualization:** Imagine desired outcomes.

2. **Affirmations:** Repeat positive statements.

3. **Gratitude Practice**: Focus on abundance.

4. **Mindful Decision-Making**: Consider karma.

Overcoming Challenges

1. **Recognize Patterns:** Identify negative patterns.

2. **Release Resistance**: Let go of attachment.

3. **Reframe Perspective**: Shift mindset.

Cultivating Positive Karma

1. **Selfless Actions**: Engage in selfless acts.

2. **Positive Intentions**: Focus on kindness, compassion.

3. **Gratitude**: Cultivate appreciation.

The Law of Attraction and *"Karma"* form a powerful synergy, empowering us to manifest reality consciously. *By understanding their interconnectedness, we can:*

1. **Shape our destiny**

2. **Overcome challenges**

3. **Cultivate spiritual growth**

Embrace this profound relationship, harnessing the potential to create a fulfilling, purpose-driven life.

It is also crucial to understand that the Law of Attraction does not work in isolation. It works in tandem with other universal principles such as the law of vibration and the law of detachment. The law of vibration states that everything in the universe is in a constant state of vibration, and our thoughts and emotions have a specific frequency that attracts similar vibrations. Therefore, it is essential to raise our vibrations through positive thoughts, feelings, and actions to attract what we desire.

Moreover, *the **law of detachment** emphasizes the importance of letting go of the outcome. When we are too attached to a specific outcome, we create resistance and block the flow of the universe.* By detaching from the outcome, we allow the universe to work its magic and manifest our desires in its own time and way.

In conclusion, the Law of Attraction and *"Karma"* are powerful universal laws that work together to shape our reality. Our thoughts and emotions attract experiences into our lives, while our actions determine the quality of those experiences. By understanding and aligning with these laws, we can manifest our desires and create a life full of abundance, joy, and fulfilment. So let us use these principles to create a positive manifesting reality for ourselves and those around us.

@@@@

CHAPTER 10

"KARMA" AND EMOTIONS: THE POWER OF THOUGHT AND INTENTION

In our daily lives, we are constantly surrounded by thoughts and emotions. Some days, we feel happy and content while on others, we may experience anger, fear, or sadness. *These emotions are a natural part of being human and can greatly influence our actions and decisions. But have you ever stopped to think about how our thoughts and intentions can impact not just our own lives, but also those around us? This is where the concept of "Karma" comes into play.*

"Karma" is a term that is commonly used in spiritual and philosophical discussions. It originates from Hinduism and Buddhism and is often referred to as the law of cause and effect. *The basic premise of "Karma" is that every action we take, every thought we have, and every intention we set has a consequence or result. In other words, what goes around comes around.*

The Power of Thought

Our thoughts are a powerful force that can shape our reality. They could dictate our emotions, actions, and our destiny. Our thoughts also have a ripple effect, impacting not just ourselves but also those around us.

For example, if you wake up in the morning with negative thoughts and a pessimistic attitude, chances are your day will not go well. Your negative energy will radiate to those you interact with, creating a chain reaction of negativity. On the other hand, *if you wake up with positive thoughts and a hopeful mindset, your day is more likely to be filled with joy and success.*

The power of thought lies in its ability to manifest into reality. When we consistently think about something, whether it is positive or negative, we attract it into our lives. This is known as the Law of Attraction – the belief that like attracts like. If you think about something long enough and with enough intensity, it will eventually manifest in your life.

Therefore, it is crucial to be mindful of our thoughts and intentionally choose the ones that serve us and those around us positively. We should aim to cultivate thoughts of love, compassion, and gratitude, as they have the power to transform our lives and the world. Emotions are of two types:

Positive Emotions

Cultivate positive emotions to create beneficial karma:

1. **Love:** Unconditional love, compassion.

2. **Gratitude:** Appreciation, thankfulness.

3. **Joy**: Happiness, positivity.

4. **Empathy**: Understanding, connection.

5. **Forgiveness**: Release resentment.

Negative Emotions

Recognize and transform negative emotions to avoid detrimental karma:

1. **Anger**: Frustration, resentment.

2. **Fear**: Anxiety, doubt.

3. **Guilt**: Regret, remorse.

4. **Jealousy**: Envy, insecurity.

5. **Hatred_** Malice, hostility.

The Impact of Intention

Our intentions are the driving force behind our thoughts and actions. They are the underlying reason for why we do what we do. The power of intention lies in its ability to give direction and purpose to our thoughts and actions.

When our intentions are pure and aligned with our values and beliefs, they can bring about positive outcomes. On the other hand, if our intentions are driven by selfish desires or negative emotions, they can lead to harmful consequences.

For instance, a person who intends to help someone out of genuine kindness will receive positive feedback and gratitude in return. But if someone's intention is to do a good deed simply for personal gain or validation, the outcome may not be as fulfilling.

In the context of *"Karma"*, our intentions also play a crucial role in shaping our future experiences. If we consistently set positive intentions, we attract positive energy and experiences into our lives. And if our intentions are driven by negative emotions such as jealousy or resentment, we will attract similar energies that may manifest as challenges or obstacles.

Thoughts and Intention

Thoughts and intentions amplify emotional energy:

1. **Mindfulness:** Awareness of thoughts, emotions.

2. **Intentional Focus:** Concentrate on positive desires.

3. **Non-Judgment:** Release attachment to outcomes.

4. **Positive Thinking**: Empowering thoughts.

5. **Clear Intentions:** Focus on specific desires.

The Power of Intention

Intention shapes *"Karma"*:

1. **Aligned Intentions:** Harmonize with universal principles.

2. **Positive Intentions:** Cultivate kindness, compassion.

3. **Clear Intentions**: Focus on specific desires.

4. **Intentional Action**: Take deliberate action.

Emotions and *"Karma"*

Our emotions are closely intertwined with both our thoughts and intentions. They are a powerful force that can either drive us towards positive or negative outcomes. Our emotions also have an impact on those around us, as they can be contagious.

For example, if we are feeling angry or frustrated, it is likely that those around us will also feel tense and uncomfortable. This creates a chain reaction of negative energy that can affect not just our immediate environment but also our future experiences.

In terms of *"Karma"*, our emotions can create a cycle of cause and effect. If we continuously hold onto negative emotions such as anger or resentment towards someone, we may unknowingly attract similar experiences in the future. This is because our emotions and thoughts are the seeds that we plant in the universe, and eventually, they will bear fruit.

Breaking the Cycle of Negative *"Karma"*

The concept of *"Karma"* may seem overwhelming, especially when we consider the impact of our thoughts, intentions, and emotions on our future experiences. But it is important to remember that *"Karma"* is not a punishment or reward system. It is simply a reminder that our actions have consequences, and we have the power to manifest positive outcomes in our lives through our thoughts and intentions.

To break the cycle of negative "Karma", we must first become aware of our thoughts and intentions. We should aim to cultivate positive thoughts and intentions that align with our values and beliefs. This could mean practicing gratitude, forgiveness, and compassion towards us and others.

We must also learn to manage our emotions effectively. Instead of suppressing or ignoring negative emotions, we should acknowledge them and find healthy ways to express and release them. This could include practicing mindfulness, journaling, or seeking professional help if needed.

Lastly, it is important to remember that *"Karma"* is a continuous cycle. Every moment presents us with an opportunity to make a conscious choice towards positive thoughts, intentions, and actions. By doing so, we can break the cycle of negative *"Karma"* and create a more fulfilling and positive life for ourselves and those around us.

Karmic Patterns

Recognize and break negative karmic patterns:

1. **Self-Awareness:** Identify patterns, emotions.

2. **Release Resistance**: Let go of attachment.

3. **Reframe Perspective**: Shift mindset.

4. **Forgiveness**: Release resentment.

Emotional Healing

Emotional healing fosters positive karma:

1. **Self-Compassion:** Cultivate empathy.

2. **Forgiveness:** Release resentment.

3. **Emotional Balance:** Stability, harmony.

4. **Mindfulness:** Awareness of thoughts, emotions.

Practical Applications

Integrate these principles into daily life:

1. **Mindfulness Meditation:** Cultivate awareness.
2. **Gratitude Practice:** Focus on abundance.
3. **Positive Affirmations**: Repeat empowering statements.
4. **Intentional Journaling:** Reflect on thoughts, emotions.

Spiritual Growth

Embracing karma and emotions fosters spiritual growth:

1. **Self-Awareness:** Understand thoughts, emotions.
2. **Personal Responsibility:** Acknowledge karma.
3. **Compassion:** Cultivate empathy.
4. **Spiritual Practice**: Meditation, yoga.

"Karma" and emotions are intertwined, influencing our reality. By understanding this dynamic relationship, we can:

1. **Harness emotional power**
2. **Cultivate positive karma**
3. **Shape our destiny**

Embrace this profound connection, harnessing emotions and thoughts to create a fulfilling, purpose-driven life.

In conclusion, the power of thought and intention plays a significant role in shaping our lives and experiences. Our thoughts, intentions, and emotions are interconnected and have a ripple effect on ourselves and others. By understanding and harnessing the power of these elements, we can break the cycle of negativity and create a more fulfilling and positive life for us and those around us. Let us choose to cultivate positive thoughts and intentions today for a better tomorrow.

@@@@

CHAPTER 11

PRACTISING "*KARMA YOGA*": SELFLESS ACTION AND SERVICE

Today, the concept of selfless action and service may seem like a foreign and outdated idea. However, the ancient Indian spiritual practice of "*Karma yoga*" teaches us the power and importance of performing actions without attachment to the results, and solely for the benefit of others. In this chapter, we will explore the principles and benefits of practicing *Karma yoga*", and how it can bring about positive changes in our personal lives and the world at large.

"*Karma Yoga*", a fundamental concept in Hindu philosophy, is the path of selfless action. It emphasizes the importance of performing duties without attachment to outcomes, cultivating detachment, and surrendering ego.

Key Principles:

1. **Selfless Action**: Perform actions without expectation of reward or personal gain.

2. **Detachment**: Let go of attachment to outcomes, success, or failure.

3. **Duty**: Fulfil duties (*swadharma*) without personal motivation.

4. **Ego Surrender**: Transcend ego and personal identity.

Philosophical Basis:

"*Karma yoga*" is rooted in the *Bhagavad Gita*, where *Lord Krishna* teaches *Arjuna* the importance of selfless action. The *Gita* emphasizes:

1. **Nishkama Karma**: Action without desire or attachment.

2. **Svadharma**: Fulfilling one's duty.

3. **Ishvara Pranidhana**: Surrendering actions to the Divine.

Benefits:

1. **Spiritual Growth**: Cultivates self-awareness, detachment.

2. **Inner Peace**: Reduces stress, anxiety.

3. **Purifies Mind**: Eliminates ego, selfishness.

Practice:

1. **Volunteer**: Engage in selfless service.

2. **Meditation**: Cultivate mindfulness, detachment.

3. **Self-Inquiry**: Reflect on motivations, actions.

"*Karma Yoga*" offers a profound path to spiritual growth, self-realization, and inner peace. By embracing selfless action and detachment, individuals can transcend ego and fulfil their duties with clarity and purpose.

What is "*Karma yoga*"?

"Karma yoga" is one of the four main paths of yoga, along with bhakti (devotion), jnana (knowledge), and raja (meditation). It is often referred to as the path of selfless action, as it emphasizes performing actions without any expectations or desires for personal gain. The word "*Karma*" itself means action, and "*yoga*" means union or connection. Therefore, "*Karma yoga*" can be seen as a practice that leads to the union with the Divine through selfless actions.

The concept of *"Karma yoga"* is deeply rooted in the Hindu philosophy of *dharma*, which refers to living a righteous and moral life. In this context, *"Karma yoga"* involves performing one's duties and responsibilities without any selfish motives or desires. It focuses on serving others and contributing to the greater good rather than seeking personal gain.

The principles of *"Karma Yoga"*

The core principle of "Karma yoga" is selflessness. It encourages individuals to act without being attached to the fruits of their actions. This means that one must focus on performing their duties to the best of their ability, without expecting any rewards or recognition in return. This detachment from results helps one to focus on the present moment and perform actions with a pure intention.

Another important principle of "Karma yoga" is performing actions with a sense of duty and responsibility. It teaches individuals to fulfil their duties and obligations towards society and humanity. This not only benefits others but also helps in personal growth and development. When we act with a sense of duty, we can overcome our ego and focus on the bigger picture rather than our individual needs.

"Karma" yoga also emphasizes the idea of surrender to a higher power. It encourages individuals to let go of their ego and trust in the divine will. This surrender allows one to detach from the outcome of their actions and have faith that everything happens for a reason. By surrendering, one can find inner peace and contentment, even in the face of challenges or failures.

The Benefits of Practicing *"Karma Yoga"*

The practice of *"Karma yoga"* brings numerous benefits to both individuals and society. Here are some of the ways in which it can positively impact our lives:

1. Development of Selflessness:

The first and most obvious benefit of practicing *"Karma yoga"* is the development of selflessness. By performing actions without any desire for personal gain, one learns to let go of their ego and focus on serving others. This helps in cultivating a sense of compassion and empathy towards others, leading to selfless actions.

2. Overcoming the Ego:

Ego is often considered the root cause of suffering and conflicts in our lives. By practicing *"Karma yoga"*, one can learn to let go of their ego and focus on the needs of others. This helps in building positive relationships and creating a harmonious environment around us.

3. Finding Inner Peace:

Our desires and attachments often lead to feelings of stress, anxiety, and discontentment. In *"Karma yoga"*, one learns to detach from these desires and focus on the present moment. This brings a sense of inner peace and contentment, leading to a happier and more fulfilling life.

4. Personal Growth:

As we perform selfless actions without any expectations, we can grow and develop on a personal level. By focusing on our duties and responsibilities, we become more disciplined, responsible, and compassionate individuals.

5. Contributing to Society:

By serving others and actively participating in the betterment of society, we can bring about positive changes in the world. *"Karma yoga"* teaches us the importance of selfless service and inspires us to contribute towards creating a more compassionate and harmonious world.

How to Incorporate "Karma yoga" in Daily Life

Incorporating ""Karma yoga" in our daily lives does not require us to make any drastic changes or sacrifices. It simply involves a shift in mindset and intention behind our actions. Here are some simple ways in which we can practice "Karma yoga":

1. Perform Random Acts of Kindness:

Small acts of kindness can go a long way in making someone's day. Simple gestures like holding the door for someone or buying a coffee for a stranger can bring joy and positivity to both the giver and receiver.

2. Volunteer:

Volunteering our time and skills for a cause or organization can be a great way to practice "Karma yoga". It allows us to serve others without any expectations and make a positive impact in our community.

3. Donate:

Donating money or resources to those in need is another way to practice "Karma yoga". By giving without expecting anything in return, we can contribute towards making a difference in someone's life.

4. Serve Others:

In our daily lives, we come across numerous opportunities to serve others, whether it is helping a colleague with a project or helping a stranger in need. By approaching these situations with a selfless attitude, we can make a positive impact on those around us.

Final Thoughts

The practice of "Karma yoga" a teaches us that true happiness lies not in personal gain but in serving others and contributing towards the greater good. It is a powerful tool for personal growth, inner peace, and building a more compassionate society. So let us all strive to incorporate the principles of *"Karma yoga"* in our daily lives and make a positive difference in the world, one selfless action at a time. As *Mahatma Gandhi* said, *"The best way to find yourself is to lose yourself in the service of others."*

@@@@

CHAPTER 12

CULTIVATING POSITIVE "*KARMA*": VIRTUES AND VALUES

"*Karma*" is a concept that has been deeply rooted in the Eastern philosophies and religions for centuries. It is the belief that our actions, thoughts, and intentions create a cosmic energy that can determine our future. In simple terms, it is the law of cause and effect - what we put out into the world, we will receive in return. However, "*Karma*" is not just about receiving what we deserve, it is also about cultivating positive energy and creating a better world for ourselves and others. This is where the concept of cultivating positive "*Karma*" through virtues and values comes into play.

Virtues and values are principles or qualities that guide our behaviour and shape our character. They are the foundation of our moral compass and influence our actions, thoughts, and intentions. By consciously cultivating positive virtues and values, we can create a ripple effect of positive energy that can have a profound impact on our lives and those around us.

Cultivating Positive "*Karma*": For Personal and Global Wellbeing

Cultivating positive "*Karma*" involves intentional actions, thoughts, and intentions that promote personal growth, well-being, and the greater good.

For Personal Wellbeing:

1. **Self-reflection:** Recognize and release negative patterns.

2. **Mindfulness:** Practice meditation, gratitude.

3. **Compassion:** Treat yourself with kindness.

4. **Positive affirmations:** Empower your mind.

5. **Selfless service:** Volunteer, help others.

For Global Welfare:

1. **Environmental stewardship**: Protect nature.

2. **Kindness and empathy**: Understand others' struggles.

3. **Social responsibility**: Engage in community service.

4. **Non-violence**: Promote peace, harmony.

5. **Interconnectedness**: Recognize unity.

Daily Practices:

1. **Morning meditation**: Set intentions.

2. **Gratitude journal:** Reflect on blessings.

3. **Random acts of kindness**: Spread joy.

4. **Eco-friendly habits**: Reduce, reuse, recycle.

5. **Prayer or mantra**: Connect with the divine.

Benefits:

1. **Inner peace**

2. **Positive relationships**

3. **Good health**

4. **Spiritual growth**

5. Contribution to global harmony

By cultivating positive *"Karma"*, we create a ripple effect of kindness, compassion, and harmony, transforming ourselves and the world.

Let us take a closer look on various virtues and values that can help us cultivate positive "Karma".

1. Kindness

Kindness is a powerful virtue that can transform lives. By being kind to ourselves and others, we are not only creating positive energy, but also contributing to a more compassionate and empathetic world. Kindness can be as simple as a smile, a kind word, or a small act of generosity. It costs nothing but has the power to make a significant difference in someone's life.

2. Gratitude

In this fast-paced world, it is easy to get caught up in the never-ending race for more. However, gratitude teaches us to appreciate what we have and be content with it. When we cultivate gratitude in our lives, we shift our focus from what we lack to what we have, thereby creating a sense of abundance. This positive mindset not only attracts more positivity into our lives but also helps us to be more giving and compassionate towards others.

3. Forgiveness

Holding onto grudges and resentment only creates negative energy within us. Forgiveness, on the other hand, is a virtue that can liberate us and help us let go of past hurts and move on. It is not about condoning or accepting wrongdoings, but rather about releasing ourselves from the burden of negative emotions. By cultivating forgiveness, we not only create positive *"Karma"* for ourselves but also contribute to a more peaceful and harmonious world.

4. Honesty

Honesty is a value that is often underrated, but its impact on our lives and those around us is immense. When we are honest in our words and actions, we build trust and integrity, which are essential for meaningful relationships. It also allows us to live an authentic life without the fear of being exposed. By cultivating honesty, we create positive *"Karma"* by staying true to ourselves and others.

5. Compassion

Compassion is the ability to understand and empathize with others' suffering and take action to alleviate it. When we cultivate compassion, we open our hearts to others and become more sensitive to their needs. This not only creates positive energy within us but also allows us to make a positive impact on the world by helping and serving those in need.

6. Respect

Respect is a value that encompasses treating others with dignity, regardless of their differences or status. When we cultivate respect, we create a harmonious environment where everyone feels valued and worthy. It also allows us to appreciate diversity and learn from different perspectives. By showing respect to others, we invite positive energy into our lives and create a more inclusive and accepting world.

7. Courage

Courage is not the absence of fear but the ability to act despite it. When we cultivate courage in our lives, we can overcome our fears and take risks for growth and progress. It also allows us to stand up for our beliefs and values, even in the face of opposition. By cultivating courage, we create positive *"Karma"* by pushing ourselves out of our comfort zones and inspiring others to do the same.

Incorporating these virtues and values into our lives can help us cultivate positive *"Karma"* and create a ripple effect of positive energy. However, it is important to remember that cultivating positive *"Karma"* is not about being perfect or always doing the right thing. It is about making a conscious effort to be better versions of ourselves and making a positive impact on the world.

In addition to these virtues and values, practicing mindfulness and self-reflection can also help us cultivate positive *"Karma"*. When we are mindful, we become more aware of our thoughts and actions, allowing us to make more conscious choices. Self-reflection also allows us to learn from our mistakes and make changes for the better.

Cultivating positive "Karma" is a continuous process that requires effort and dedication. But the rewards are immeasurable. By incorporating these virtues and values into our lives, we not only create positive energy for ourselves but also contribute to a more compassionate, peaceful, and harmonious world. So let us all make a conscious effort to cultivate positive *"Karma"* through our virtues and values and make this world a better place for ourselves and future generations.

@@@@

CHAPTER 13

OVERCOMING NEGATIVE *"KARMA"*: FORGIVENESS AND RELEASE

"Karma", a concept derived from ancient Indian spiritual beliefs, refers to the law of cause and effect. It states that every action we take, whether good or bad, will have a corresponding consequence. This belief suggests that our actions in this lifetime are influenced by our past actions and that we are responsible for creating our own destiny.

While many people associate *"Karma"* with the idea of punishment for wrongdoing, it is important to understand that it is not solely about retribution. It is also about learning and growth. Negative *"Karma"* can manifest in various ways, such as experiencing challenges, obstacles, and setbacks in life. These experiences can be seen as opportunities for us to reflect on our actions and make changes for the better.

However, at times, it may seem like we are stuck in a never-ending cycle of negative *"Karma"*. No matter how much we try to do good and make amends, we continue to face hardships and difficulties. *In such situations, it can be easy to feel discouraged and overwhelmed. But the key to breaking this cycle lies in two powerful practices: forgiveness and release.*

Forgiveness is the act of pardoning someone who has wronged us, while release is letting go of any negative feelings or attachments towards a person or situation. These practices may seem simple, but they hold immense power in helping us overcome negative "Karma".

Let us look deeper into how forgiveness and release can help us break the cycle of negative *"Karma"*:

1. Forgiveness brings inner peace

When we hold grudges, resentment, or anger towards someone who has wronged us, we are hurting ourselves more than anyone else. These negative emotions create a heavy burden on our hearts and minds, leading to stress, anxiety, and other health issues.

By forgiving others for their wrongdoings, we release ourselves from this burden and find inner peace. It allows us to let go of the negative energy associated with the situation and move forward with a lighter heart and a clearer mind. In doing so, we also free ourselves from any negative *"Karma"* that may have been attached to the situation.

2. Release helps us detach from the past

The past can be a powerful and relentless force, especially when it comes to negative experiences. We may find ourselves holding onto past hurts, regrets, and traumas, which can weigh us down and hinder our growth. Release is about learning to detach from these past experiences and not letting them define us.

By releasing ourselves from the past, we can break free from the cycle of negative *"Karma"* associated with it. We can let go of any self-limiting beliefs or patterns that may be holding us back and open ourselves up to new opportunities for growth and positive experiences.

3. Forgiveness and release promote empathy and understanding

Forgiveness and release are not just about letting go of negative feelings towards others, but also about developing empathy and understanding. By forgiving others, we learn to put ourselves in their shoes and understand their perspective. This practice helps us see things from a different angle, which can lead to healing and reconciliation.

Similarly, by releasing ourselves from negative attachments towards a person or situation, we can cultivate a greater sense of understanding for others and their actions. This allows us to break free from any negative *"Karma"* associated with our own actions towards others.

4. They help us take responsibility for our actions

As mentioned earlier, *"Karma"* is about cause and effect. Therefore, it is important for us to take responsibility for our actions and their consequences. By forgiving others, we also acknowledge our own role in the situation and take responsibility for our reactions towards it.

Similarly, by releasing ourselves from past traumas and attachments, we also take responsibility for how they have affected us and make a conscious effort to move forward in a positive direction. This act of taking responsibility can help us break the cycle of negative *"Karma"* and create a more positive future for ourselves.

5. Forgiveness and release open us up to abundance and positivity

Negative *"Karma"* can often feel like a dark cloud that follows us wherever we go. It can make us feel stuck and prevent us from experiencing abundance and positivity in our lives. By practicing forgiveness and release, we open ourselves up to new opportunities and experiences that we may have been blocking ourselves from.

When we let go of negative attachments and emotions, we create space for positivity, love, and abundance to enter our lives. We also attract good "Karma" by letting go of any resentment or grudges towards others, which can lead to more positive relationships and experiences.

In conclusion, forgiveness and release are powerful practices that can help us break the cycle of negative *"Karma"* in our lives. They allow us to let go of past hurts, take responsibility for our actions, and open ourselves up to new opportunities for growth and positive experiences. So, the next time you find yourself facing difficulties and challenges, remember to practice forgiveness and release to break free from the cycle of negative *"Karma"* and create a brighter future for yourself.

@@@@

CHAPTER 14

KARMA AND RELATIONSHIPS: INTERCONNECTEDNESS AND RESPONSIBILITY

Relationships are an integral part of our lives. Be it with our family, friends, or romantic partners, we constantly seek meaningful connections with others. These relationships bring us joy, comfort, and support, but they can also bring challenges and conflicts. *While we may attribute these ups and downs to various factors, one aspect that often goes unnoticed is the role of "Karma" in our relationships.*

"Karma" is a concept that has been around for centuries and is deeply embedded in various spiritual and philosophical beliefs. It is often associated with the idea of cause and effect, where our actions in this life determine our future experiences. *In the context of relationships, "Karma" refers to the interconnectedness and responsibility we have towards the people in our lives.*

Interconnectedness in Relationships

The notion of interconnectedness suggests that everything in this world is connected in one way or another. In the case of relationships, it means that every person we encounter has a purpose in our lives. They are not merely chance encounters but rather a part of our journey towards self-discovery and growth.

When we view relationships through the lens of interconnectedness, we start to see them as opportunities for learning and evolution. Every person we meet teaches us something about ourselves, whether it is about our strengths, weaknesses, triggers, or desires. For instance, a difficult boss may teach us patience and resilience, while a supportive friend may remind us of our capacity for love and compassion.

Moreover, *our actions and words in a relationship have a ripple effect on others. If we are kind and loving towards someone, they are likely to reciprocate those feelings and spread positivity to others. On the other hand, if we are hurtful and negative, it can create a cycle of pain and suffering.* This interdependence highlights the importance of being mindful of our thoughts, words, and actions towards others.

Taking Responsibility for Our Relationships

"Karma" also teaches us the concept of responsibility in relationships. It reminds us that we are not mere passive participants in our relationships but active creators of our experiences. Our actions and choices in a relationship have consequences and can influence the quality of our connections.

Often, we tend to blame others for the challenges and conflicts in our relationships. We may attribute it to their behaviour, personality, or past experiences. While these factors may play a role, it is essential to acknowledge our role in creating or contributing to the situation.

For instance, if we constantly criticize our partner and fail to express gratitude for their efforts, it is likely to create resentment and distance in the relationship. In this scenario, it is crucial to take responsibility for our words and actions and make efforts to improve the dynamics of the relationship.

Moreover, *understanding the concept of "Karma" can also help us take responsibility for healing and improving our relationships. If we have hurt someone in the past, acknowledging our mistakes and making amends can help us move towards forgiveness and reconciliation.* It also encourages us to let go of grudges and past hurts, which can hinder the growth of a relationship.

Breaking Karmic Patterns in Relationships

In some cases, we may find ourselves stuck in unhealthy relationships that are repeating the same patterns repeatedly. These patterns are often referred to as *karmic* cycles, where we keep encountering similar situations or people until we learn the lessons they are meant to teach us.

For instance, *if we constantly find ourselves in toxic relationships, it could be an indication that we need to work on setting healthy boundaries and valuing ourselves more.* Until we learn this lesson, we may continue to attract similar experiences. By understanding the role of *"Karma"* in our relationships, we can break these cycles and move towards healthier connections.

"Karma" also teaches us that every relationship serves a purpose. Even if it ends on a sour note, it may have taught us valuable lessons and helped us grow. It is essential to let go of any resentment or bitterness towards past relationships and instead focus on the lessons we have learned.

Cultivating Positive *"Karma"* in Relationships

While *"Karma"* may seem like a complex concept, it comes down to the simple principle of treating others how we want to be treated. In the context of relationships, this means showing love, kindness, and understanding towards those we care about.

Furthermore, cultivating positive *"Karma"* in our relationships also involves being mindful of our intentions behind our actions. Are we doing something out of genuine love and care, or are we seeking something in return? By constantly examining our intentions, we can ensure that our actions are aligned with creating positive energy and harmony in our relationships.

In addition, *practicing empathy and forgiveness can also help us build positive "Karma" in our relationships. By putting ourselves in someone else's shoes and understanding their perspective, we can foster deeper connections and avoid conflicts. And when conflicts do arise, forgiveness can help us release any negative energy and move towards healing and growth.*

In conclusion, understanding the role of *"Karma"* in our relationships can bring a significant shift in how we approach and nurture them. By acknowledging the interconnectedness and responsibility we have towards others, we can create more meaningful and fulfilling connections. Moreover, by breaking karmic patterns and cultivating positive *"Karma"*, we can build stronger and healthier relationships that contribute to our overall growth and well-being. So, let us embrace the concept of *"Karma"* and use it as a guiding force in our relationships.

@@@@

CHAPTER 15

"*KARMA*" AND SPIRITUAL EVOLUTION: SOUL GROWTH AND TRANSFORMATION

"*Karma*" is a term that is commonly used in spiritual and philosophical discussions, but it is often misunderstood and misinterpreted. It is a concept that has its roots in Hinduism and Buddhism, but it has been adopted and integrated into various other belief systems and religions. In simple terms, "*Karma*" refers to the law of cause and effect – the idea that our actions, thoughts, and intentions have consequences that determine our future experiences. In this chapter, we will look deeper into the concept of "*Karma*" and explore its role in spiritual evolution, specifically in terms of soul growth and transformation.

"*Karma*" and Soul Growth

"Karma" plays a vital role in our spiritual evolution as it is closely tied to the growth of our soul. Our souls are eternal beings on a journey of growth and self-discovery. Each lifetime presents us with opportunities for growth and learning, and our karmic experiences are the lessons we must learn to evolve spiritually.

When we experience challenges or difficulties in life, it is often a result of our past actions or thoughts. These experiences serve as opportunities for us to learn and grow, to correct any negative past actions, and to create positive "*Karma*" for ourselves. The law of "*Karma*" ensures that we are accountable for our actions and that we have the power to shape our future experiences through the choices we make in the present.

Transformation through "*Karma*"

"Karma" has the power to transform us – not only in terms of our spiritual evolution but also in our day-to-day lives. By understanding and accepting the concept of "Karma", we can become more mindful of our actions and intentions, leading to more positive outcomes in our lives.

When we experience negative consequences due to past actions or intentions, we can reflect, learn, and make amends. This process of self-reflection and growth can lead to a transformation in our thoughts, beliefs, and behaviour. Through the law of "Karma", we can break free from negative patterns and create a more positive future for ourselves.

Breaking the Cycle

"Karma" is often described as a wheel that keeps turning – what goes around comes around. This is because when we do not learn our lessons and continue to engage in negative actions, we create a karmic cycle that keeps repeating itself. However, *"Karma" also offers us a way out – by breaking this cycle through conscious actions and intentions.*

When we make a conscious effort to create positive *"Karma"* through selfless actions and intentions, we can break free from negative cycles and create a brighter future for ourselves. This is how *"Karma"* can lead to spiritual transformation – by helping us let go of negative patterns and behaviours and guiding us towards a more enlightened way of being.

The Importance of Intention

In the concept of *"Karma"*, intention plays a significant role. *It is not just our actions that determine our karmic consequences but also the intentions behind those actions. If our intentions are pure and selfless, the karmic consequences will be positive. On the other hand, if our intentions are selfish and harmful, the karmic consequences will be negative.*

Therefore, it is essential to be mindful of our intentions and to cultivate positive intentions in all aspects of our lives. By doing so, we can create a ripple effect of positivity and contribute to our own spiritual growth and that of others around us.

"Karma" in Different Belief Systems

Although *"Karma"* is most associated with Hinduism and Buddhism, similar concepts can be found in various other belief systems and religions. In Christianity, the concept of *"you reap what you sow"* is closely related to *"Karma"*. In Islam, the principle of *"as you sow, so shall you reap"* also aligns with the concept of *"Karma"*.

The underlying idea in all these belief systems is that our actions have consequences and that we are responsible for our choices. This emphasizes the universal nature of the concept of *"Karma"* and its importance in shaping our lives and spiritual evolution.

Final Thoughts

In conclusion, "Karma" is an essential concept in spiritual evolution as it teaches us about the power of our actions and intentions. It reminds us that we are accountable for our choices and that we can shape our future through conscious actions and thoughts. By understanding and embracing *"Karma"*, we can break free from negative patterns and behaviours, leading us towards soul growth and transformation. Let us strive to create positive *"Karma"* in all aspects of our lives and contribute to a more enlightened world.

@@@@

CHAPTER 16

THE ROLE OF MINDFULNESS AND MEDITATION IN *"KARMA"*

In the fast-paced world, it is easy to get caught up in the daily hustle and bustle and forget about the importance of mindfulness and meditation. However, these practices have been around for centuries and have many benefits, including their role in *"Karma", which* is a concept that has deep roots in Eastern philosophy and is often associated with ideas of fate and destiny. In this chapter, we will explore the relationship between mindfulness, meditation, and *"Karma"* and how they work together to create a more fulfilling and purposeful life.

To understand the role of mindfulness and meditation in *"Karma"*, we first need to define what *"Karma"* means. In Sanskrit, *"Karma"* translates to *"action"* or *"deed"* and refers to the universal law that every action has a consequence. This means that every thought, word, and action we take has an impact on our future experiences. It is the belief that our past actions determine our present circumstances, and our present actions will shape our future.

Now, **how do mindfulness and meditation play a part in this concept?** Mindfulness is the practice of being fully present in the moment, without judgment or distraction. It involves paying attention to our thoughts, feelings, and surroundings without getting caught up in them. On the other hand, meditation is a practice of training the mind to achieve a state of consciousness that is calm, focused, and relaxed. Both mindfulness and meditation help us cultivate a deeper understanding of ourselves, our actions, and their consequences – all essential elements of *"Karma"*.

One way in which **mindfulness** contributes to *"Karma"* is through the awareness it brings to our thoughts and actions. Often, we go through our day on autopilot, reacting impulsively without considering the consequences of our actions. This can lead to negative outcomes and create negative karmic patterns. *By practicing mindfulness, we become more attuned to our thoughts and emotions. We can then make more conscious and intentional decisions, leading to more positive actions and outcomes.*

Similarly, **meditation** *allows us to tune out the distractions of the outside world and focus on our inner selves. It helps us to quiet our minds, observe our thoughts, and gain a better understanding of our actions and their consequences.* Through regular meditation practice, we can become more aware of our habitual patterns and tendencies, such as negative thoughts and reactions. By acknowledging these patterns, we can work towards changing them and creating more positive karmic cycles.

Moreover, *mindfulness and meditation also help us to cultivate compassion towards ourselves and others. When we are mindful, we become more empathetic towards others' suffering and develop a deeper understanding of their actions. This leads us to approach situations with kindness and compassion rather than judgment and resentment.* Similarly, meditation allows us to let go of negative emotions such as anger, jealousy, and greed that can lead to negative karmic consequences. By practicing compassion and letting go of negative emotions, we create positive energy that can break negative karmic cycles.

Another essential aspect of "Karma" is the idea of intention or volition – the motivation behind our actions. In Buddhism, it is believed that one's intentions determine the moral value of an action. Mindfulness helps us to become aware of our intentions by bringing attention to our thoughts before turning them into actions. By being mindful of our intentions, we can ensure that they align with our values and beliefs, leading to a more positive karmic impact.

Furthermore, both mindfulness and meditation have been linked to an increase in self-awareness and self-reflection. These practices allow us to look inward, reflect on our past actions, and identify any negative patterns or behaviours that may contribute to negative *"Karma"*. By acknowledging and working on these patterns, we can break negative cycles and create more positive karmic outcomes.

In conclusion, mindfulness and meditation play a significant role in *"Karma"* by helping us become more aware and intentional in our actions. They allow us to cultivate compassion, let go of negative emotions, and become more self-aware, all of which contribute to creating positive karmic cycles. By incorporating these practices into our daily lives, we can lead a more mindful and intentional existence and create a brighter future for ourselves and those around us.

So, the next time you find yourself caught up in the chaos of modern life, take a moment to pause and practice mindfulness or meditation. Not only will it bring peace and clarity to your present moment, but it will also contribute to creating positive *"Karma"* in your life. Remember, every small action counts, and by being mindful and intentional, we can create a ripple effect of positivity in the world.

@@@

CHAPTER 17

BREAKING FREE FROM *"KARMIC"* PATTERNS: LIBERATION AND ENLIGHTENMENT

"Karma", a concept deeply rooted in Hinduism and Buddhism, has long been associated with the idea of cause and effect. It is the belief that our actions, thoughts, and intentions create a cycle of consequences that shape our present and future lives. This cycle is known as karmic patterns, and it is believed to be the force that governs our existence. However, is it possible to break free from these patterns and attain liberation and enlightenment? In this chapter, we will explore the concept of *karmic* patterns and how we can break free from them to achieve true liberation and enlightenment.

Understanding *Karmic* Patterns

To understand karmic patterns, we must first understand the concept of *"Karma"*. *"Karma"* is the accumulation of actions, both good and bad, that determine our future experiences. According to Eastern philosophy, every action we take creates an imprint on our soul, which will eventually manifest in our present or future lives. This continuous cycle of cause and effect is known as samsara, or the wheel of life.

Karmic patterns are formed when we repeatedly engage in certain actions or behaviours, creating a habit or a pattern. For example, if we consistently act with anger towards others, we will attract situations and people that trigger our anger. This pattern will continue until we break the cycle by changing our behaviour. The same goes for positive actions – if we consistently practice kindness and compassion, we will attract similar experiences into our lives.

Breaking Free from Karmic Patterns

The idea of breaking free from karmic patterns may seem daunting at first. How can we escape something that is an inevitable part of our existence? The key lies in understanding the root cause of these patterns – our thoughts and beliefs.

Our thoughts and beliefs are powerful creators of our reality. They shape our perceptions, attitudes, and actions. If we hold onto negative thoughts and beliefs, we will continue to manifest negative experiences in our lives. Therefore, *to break free from karmic patterns, we must first address and transform our thoughts and beliefs.*

The process of breaking free from karmic patterns involves self-reflection and inner work. We must take an honest look at our thoughts and beliefs and identify any patterns that may be limiting us. This requires us to be open-minded and willing to let go of old beliefs that no longer serve us.

Practicing mindfulness is an effective way to become aware of our thoughts and break free from negative patterns. By being present in the moment, we can observe our thoughts without judgment and consciously choose to let go of any negative patterns that arise.

Additionally, *cultivating self-love and compassion towards us is crucial in breaking free from karmic patterns. Often, these patterns are formed due to past traumas or insecurities, and by showing ourselves love and compassion, we can heal these wounds and transform our actions.*

The Role of Liberation and Enlightenment

Breaking free from karmic patterns is not just about creating a better life for ourselves. It is also an essential step towards attaining liberation and enlightenment. *Liberation refers to the freedom from the cycle of birth and death, while enlightenment is the state of ultimate spiritual awakening.*

Karmic patterns keep us trapped in the cycle of *samsara*, preventing us from reaching a state of liberation and enlightenment. By breaking these patterns, we can break free from the limitations of our human existence and reach a higher state of consciousness.

Enlightenment also involves detachment from desires and attachments. Karmic patterns are often driven by our desires and attachments, as we continuously seek external validation or fulfilment. By breaking free from these patterns, we can detach ourselves from these desires and attachments, allowing us to experience true inner peace and contentment.

Practical Steps for Breaking Free

Breaking free from karmic patterns is a journey that requires dedication, self-reflection, and inner work. However, there are practical steps that we can take to aid us in this process.

1. Practice Self-Awareness:

As mentioned earlier, being mindful of our thoughts and actions is crucial in breaking free from karmic patterns. By practicing self-awareness, we can identify any negative patterns and consciously choose to change them.

2. Cultivate Compassion:

As we work towards breaking free from these patterns, we may encounter challenges and setbacks. It is important to show ourselves compassion and understanding during this process. Remember, it is a journey, and it is okay to make mistakes.

3. Let Go of the Past:

Karmic patterns are often rooted in past traumas or experiences. It is essential to let go of the past and not let it define our present and future. By releasing any attachment to the past, we can create space for new, positive experiences.

4. Practice Forgiveness:

Holding onto grudges or resentments towards others only perpetuates negative karmic patterns. By practicing forgiveness, we can release ourselves from these patterns and create healthier relationships with others.

5. Trust the Process:

Breaking free from karmic patterns takes time and effort. It is crucial to trust the process and have faith that we are on the right path towards liberation and enlightenment.

In conclusion, breaking free from karmic patterns is a journey of self-discovery and transformation. By understanding the root cause of these patterns and taking practical steps to break them, we can attain liberation and enlightenment. It is a continuous process that requires dedication, but the rewards are immeasurable – true inner peace, contentment, and spiritual awakening. So let us all take the first step towards breaking free from our karmic patterns and embrace a life of liberation and enlightenment.

@@@@

CHAPTER 18

"KARMA" AND THE PATH TO SELF-REALISATION

"Karma" is a concept that has been widely discussed and debated in various spiritual beliefs and philosophical traditions. It is often used to explain the idea of cause and effect, the cycle of birth and rebirth, and the concept of destiny. In simple terms, *"Karma"* can be understood as the energy that we create through our thoughts, actions, and intentions, which eventually shapes our present and future experiences. However, its true essence goes beyond this basic understanding. In this chapter, we will look deeper into the concept of *"Karma"* and explore its connection with the path to self-realization.

The word "Karma" comes from the Sanskrit word *'kr'* which means 'to do' or 'to act'. It refers to the actions that we perform in our daily lives, both consciously and unconsciously. These actions create an energy that is imprinted on our consciousness and affects our future experiences. It is often described as a law of cause and effect, where every action has a corresponding reaction or consequence.

According to Hinduism, Buddhism, and Jainism, *"Karma"* is not just limited to one lifetime but carries over from one life to another. This belief in reincarnation is based on the idea that our actions in one lifetime determine our destiny in the next. This cycle of birth and rebirth continues until we break free from the cycle by achieving self-realization or enlightenment.

So, what exactly is self-realization and how does it relate to *"Karma"*? Self-realization can be defined as the discovery of one's true self beyond the ego-mind. It is the realization that we are not just physical beings, but also spiritual beings connected to a higher consciousness. This understanding brings about a deep sense of inner peace and fulfilment.

Now, let us look at how *"Karma"* plays a role in our journey towards self-realization. Our actions are heavily influenced by our thoughts and beliefs. We all have desires, fears, and attachments that drive us to act in certain ways. These desires and attachments create a karmic cycle, where we keep repeating the same patterns and experiences until we learn the lessons they hold for us.

For example, if we have a desire to be wealthy and successful, we may take actions that are driven by greed or selfishness. This creates a karmic energy that will eventually manifest in our lives, either positively or negatively. If we continue to chase this desire without considering its consequences, we may end up experiencing financial difficulties or losing relationships due to our selfish behaviours. This is where the concept of *"Karma"* comes into play – our actions and intentions create an energy that shapes our future experiences.

On the path to self-realization, it is essential to become aware of our karmic patterns and understand their root causes. By doing so, we can break free from the cycle of repetitive behaviours and experiences. This requires introspection and self-reflection – reflecting on our actions and thoughts, understanding their motivations, and questioning whether they align with our true selves or are driven by our ego-driven desires.

As we become more aware of our karmic patterns, we can make conscious choices to let go of old thought patterns and behaviours that no longer serve us. This process of letting go and breaking free from *karmic* cycles is not easy, but it is necessary for our growth and self-realization. It requires courage, determination, and a willingness to face our shadows and let go of our attachments.

Along with breaking free from *karmic* cycles, another crucial aspect of the path to self-realization is living in alignment with one's *dharma*. *Dharma* refers to one's true purpose or calling in life. It is often described as one's unique role or contribution to the world. When we live in alignment with our *dharma*, we are living in harmony with the universe and our true selves, thus reducing the creation of negative "Karma".

On the other hand, *living against our dharma can lead to feelings of emptiness, discontentment, and a sense of being out of alignment with our true selves. This can create a karmic cycle of negative experiences, as we are not living in alignment with the natural flow of our lives.*

In addition to being aware of our karmic patterns and living in alignment with our dharma, practicing mindfulness and cultivating positive thoughts and intentions can also lead us towards self-realization. Mindfulness allows us to be present in the moment and observe our thoughts and actions without judgment. Through this practice, we can become more aware of our thoughts and choose to replace negative or harmful thoughts with more positive ones.

Similarly, *cultivating positive intentions such as love, compassion, and selflessness can also help us on our journey towards self-realization. These intentions create a positive karmic energy that can lead to more fulfilling and harmonious experiences.*

In conclusion, "Karma" and the path to self-realization are deeply intertwined. Our actions and intentions create a karmic energy that shapes our future experiences, while self-realization allows us to break free from negative karmic cycles and live in alignment with our true selves. By becoming aware of our karmic patterns, living in alignment with our dharma, and cultivating mindfulness and positive intentions, we can pave the way for self-realization and a more fulfilling life. As the famous quote by *Mahatma Gandhi* goes, "The best way to find yourself is to lose yourself in the service of others." Let us strive towards selflessness and self-realization on our journey towards a more fulfilling life.

@@@@

CHAPTER 19

INTEGRATING "KARMA" INTO DAILY LIFE: PRACTICAL TIPS AND STRATEGIES

"Karma", a concept rooted in Hinduism and Buddhism, is often misunderstood and misinterpreted in modern society. Many people associate *"Karma"* with the idea of *"what goes around comes around"* or as a form of cosmic punishment for our actions. However, "Karma" is much more than that. *It is the law of cause and effect, the understanding that our thoughts, words, and actions have consequences that shape our present and future experiences.*

Integrating *"Karma"* into daily life is not about living in fear of repercussions or trying to be perfect. It is about cultivating a deeper sense of awareness and responsibility for our thoughts and actions. It is about living with intention and aligning ourselves with the flow of the universe. In this chapter, we will explore some practical tips and strategies for incorporating the concept of *"Karma"* into our daily lives.

1. Practice Mindfulness

The first step to integrating *"Karma"* into daily life is to cultivate mindfulness, which is the practice of being present in the moment, aware of our thoughts, feelings, and actions without judgment. By practicing mindfulness, we can become more aware of our thoughts and intentions and how they may impact ourselves and others.

Mindfulness also helps us break free from automatic reactions and patterns, allowing us to respond to situations with more thoughtfulness. This can prevent us from acting impulsively and creating negative *"Karma"* for ourselves.

2. Understand the Law of Cause and Effect

"Karma" can be simplified as the law of cause and effect – every action we take has a consequence, whether positive or negative. Understanding this concept can help us become more mindful of our choices and their potential impact.

We can start by reflecting on our past actions and their consequences.

Did we act with good intentions?

How did others react?

This self-reflection can help us become more aware of our patterns and make changes for the better.

3. Cultivate Positive Thoughts and Intentions

Our thoughts and intentions are powerful. They shape our actions, which in turn create our reality. *By cultivating positive thoughts and intentions, we can create positive "Karma" for ourselves.*

Negative thoughts and intentions, such as jealousy, anger, and greed, can lead to negative actions and create negative "Karma". By shifting our mindset to one of kindness, compassion, and gratitude, we can attract more positivity into our lives.

4. Take Responsibility for Your Actions

One of the key principles of "Karma" is taking responsibility for our actions. It is easy to blame others or external factors for our circumstances, but true growth and transformation come from accepting responsibility for our choices.

By taking ownership of our actions, we can learn from our mistakes and make better choices in the future. This not only creates positive "Karma" but also helps us become more self-aware and accountable.

5. Practice non-attachment

"Karma" also teaches us the importance of non-attachment. *Non-attachment does not mean detachment or apathy. It means letting go of our expectations and desires for a certain outcome.* When we are too attached to a specific outcome, we may become disappointed or resentful if things do not turn out as we planned.

By practicing non-attachment, we can let go of the need to control every situation and trust in the universe's flow. This can help us release any negative emotions that may arise from unmet expectations.

6. Act with Kindness and Compassion

Acts of kindness and compassion not only create positive *"Karma"* but also bring joy and fulfilment into our lives. *By treating others with kindness and empathy, we can create a ripple effect of positivity in the world.*

This does not mean we have to go out of our way to do grand gestures; even small acts of kindness – like holding the door open for someone or offering a smile – can make a difference in someone's day.

7. Reflect on Your Actions at the End of Each Day

At the end of each day, take a few moments to reflect on your thoughts, words, and actions:

Did you act with good intentions?

Did you harm anyone?

Did you make choices that aligned with your values?

This practice of self-reflection can help us become more mindful and adjust for the future. It can also serve to track our progress and see how far we have come in our journey towards integrating *"Karma"* into our daily lives.

8. Let Go of Grudges and Forgiveness

Holding onto grudges and resentments only creates negative *"Karma"* for ourselves. It can also weigh us down and prevent us from moving forward.

Forgiveness, on the other hand, is a powerful tool for releasing negative emotions and creating positive *"Karma"*. *This does not mean we condone harmful behaviour, but rather we choose to let go of the negative energy associated with it.*

9. Practice Self-Care

Integrating "Karma" into daily life also means taking care of ourselves. When we neglect our physical, mental, and emotional well-being, it can have a ripple effect on our actions and thoughts.

Be available for self-care activities like exercise, meditation, spending time in nature, or pursuing hobbies that bring you joy. When we nourish ourselves, we can show up as the best versions of ourselves in the world.

In conclusion, integrating *"Karma"* into daily life is a journey that requires effort and self-reflection. It is about being mindful of our thoughts, intentions, and actions and taking responsibility for their consequences. By cultivating kindness, compassion, and mindfulness, we can create positive *"Karma"* for ourselves and those around us. Remember that *"Karma"* is not about being perfect but about striving to do better every day. So let us all strive to live with intention and align ourselves with the flow of the universe.

@@@@

CHAPTER 20

THE FUTURE OF "KARMA": EVOLVING CONSCIOUSNESS AND GLOBAL RESPONSIBILITY

"Karma", a concept deeply rooted in the Eastern philosophies and religions, has been gaining attention in the Western world in recent years. Often misunderstood as a punishment or reward system, *"Karma"* is much more than that. It is a powerful force that governs our actions, thoughts, and shapes our lives. *As we continue to evolve as a society and face numerous global challenges, the concept of "Karma" has taken on a new significance in shaping the future of humanity. In this chapter, we will explore the future of "Karma" and its role in evolving consciousness and global responsibility.*

To understand the future of *"Karma"*, we must first understand its true meaning. *"Karma"* is derived from the Sanskrit word *"kr,"* which means action or deed. It refers to the universal law of cause and effect, where every action we take has a consequence that we will face. This concept is not limited to just our individual actions but also encompasses our thoughts and intentions. In other words, *"Karma" is the energy created by our choices, both good and bad, which will eventually come back to us in some form or another.*

Today individualism and instant gratification are highly valued, the concept of *"Karma"* may seem outdated or even irrelevant. However, as we continue to face global challenges such as climate change, social injustice, and political turmoil, the relevance of *"Karma"* becomes more apparent. Our actions and choices have far-reaching consequences that not only affect us but also impact the world around us. Therefore, understanding the power of our *"Karma"* is crucial for creating a positive impact on a global scale.

One area where "Karma" is playing a significant role in shaping the future is in our collective consciousness. As we become more connected through technology and social media, we are also becoming more aware of global issues and injustices. This increased awareness is leading to a shift in consciousness, where people are beginning to recognize the interconnectedness of all beings and the impact of their actions on others. This shift is rooted in the principles of "Karma", as it highlights the interdependence of our actions and their consequences on a larger scale.

The future of *"Karma"* also extends to our sense of global responsibility. As our actions have a ripple effect on the world around us, it is crucial for us to take responsibility for our choices and their impact. This means being mindful of our actions and actively working towards creating positive change in the world. We can no longer turn a blind eye to global issues and simply focus on our individual needs and desires. As the saying goes, *"we rise by lifting others," and this sentiment is at the core of understanding and embracing the concept of "Karma".*

Moreover, as we continue to evolve as a society, our understanding of *"Karma"* is also evolving. *While traditional beliefs view "Karma" as a linear cause and effect system, modern interpretations recognize that it is much more complex and dynamic. The law of "Karma" is not just limited to this lifetime but also extends to past lives and future lives. This means that our actions not only affect us in the present but also have long-term consequences that we may not fully understand.*

In addition to individual "Karma", there is also collective "Karma", which refers to the accumulated actions and energy of a group or society. This concept is particularly significant in today's world, where we are facing global challenges that require collective efforts and responsibility. Our collective "Karma" as a society has played a role in creating these challenges, and it is up to us to take responsibility and work towards resolving them.

So, what does the future hold for *"Karma"*?

As we continue to evolve as a society and face various challenges, the concept of *"Karma"* will play an increasingly important role in shaping our actions and consciousness. It will guide us towards making more mindful choices that not only benefit ourselves but also benefit the world around us. The future of *"Karma"* is one where we take responsibility for our actions and work towards creating a more compassionate and just world for all beings.

In conclusion, the concept of *"Karma"* is much more than just a reward and punishment system. It is a powerful force that governs our actions and has a significant impact on our individual and collective consciousness. As we continue to evolve as a society and face global challenges, the understanding and acceptance of *"Karma"* will be crucial in shaping a better future for humanity. Let us embrace the power of our *"Karma"* and work towards creating a more conscious and responsible world.

@@@@

CHAPTER 21

CONCLUSION: EMBRACING THE LAW OF *"KARMA"*

To truly embrace the Law of *"Karma"*, we must first understand its core principles. *One of the fundamental aspects of "Karma" is that it is not just about our actions but also about our intentions behind those actions.* This means that even if we do something good, but with harmful intentions, it will still bring about negative consequences. Similarly, if we do something that may seem wrong, but with good intentions, it will bring about positive results.

Another crucial aspect of "Karma" is that it is not just limited to this lifetime. The law of cause and effect extends beyond our current existence and applies to past and future lives as well. This belief is deeply ingrained in Hinduism and Buddhism, where the concept of reincarnation is prevalent. It suggests that our actions in this life will determine our experiences in the next life. This understanding brings a sense of accountability for our actions and decisions.

Embracing the Law of "Karma" can have a profound impact on our lives. It can help us make more conscious choices and take responsibility for our actions. As we begin to understand the concept of cause and effect, we can start to let go of blaming others for our circumstances and take control of our destiny.

One way to apply the Law of *"Karma"* in our daily lives is by practicing mindfulness. Mindfulness involves being present in the moment and being aware of our thoughts, actions, and intentions. By being mindful, we can catch ourselves before making impulsive decisions or acting out of negative emotions. This allows us to make conscious choices that align with our values and beliefs, therefore creating positive *"Karma"* for ourselves.

Furthermore, embracing the Law of *"Karma"* can also help us let go of resentment and grudges towards others. When we understand that every action has a consequence, we can start to have compassion for those who have wronged us. This does not mean we condone their actions, but rather we can forgive and move on from the situation. This act of forgiveness can bring about a sense of peace and release the negative energy that may be holding us back.

Moreover, the Law of *"Karma"* teaches us to take responsibility for our own happiness. It reminds us that our actions and decisions shape our experiences. We cannot control everything that happens to us, but we can control how we react to it. By accepting this, we can let go of victim mentality and take charge of our lives.

Embracing the Law of "Karma" also means understanding that everyone is on their own journey. We may not always understand why certain things happen to us or others, but it is all part of the grand plan of cause and effect. This understanding can bring about a sense of peace and acceptance, allowing us to focus on our own growth and journey without comparing it to others.

In addition to its impact on individuals, the Law of "Karma" also extends to society. If more people start embracing this universal principle, we can create a more harmonious and just world. Our actions have a ripple effect, and by cultivating positive *"Karma",* we can contribute to a more compassionate and interconnected society.

In conclusion, the Law of *"Karma"* is not just a religious concept but a universal principle that applies to all aspects of our lives. By embracing it, we can gain a deeper understanding of ourselves and our place in the world. It teaches us to be mindful, take responsibility for our actions, and let go of negative emotions. It also reminds us of the interconnectedness of all beings and the impact we have on each other.

So let us embrace the Law of *"Karma"* and create a better world for ourselves and others.

@@@@

CHAPTER 22

A GLOSSARY OF *"KARMA"*-RELATED TERMS

"Karma" is a concept that has been deeply ingrained in various cultures and religions for centuries. Let us dive into the world of "Karma" and unpack some of the key concepts and terms associated with it.

1. *"Karma"*

"Karma", in its simplest form, refers to the concept of cause and effect. It is believed that our actions, thoughts, and intentions create a ripple effect, which eventually determines our destiny. Positive actions lead to positive outcomes, while negative actions result in negative consequences.

2. *Dharma*

"Dharma" is often used interchangeably with *"Karma"*, but it has a slightly different meaning. It refers to the moral and ethical duties and responsibilities that one must fulfil in their lifetime. It is believed that by following one's *dharma*, one can accumulate good *"Karma"* and eventually reach enlightenment.

3. *Samsara*

Samsara refers to the cycle of birth, death, and rebirth in Hinduism and Buddhism. It is believed that our actions in this life will determine our next life – whether we will be reborn into a higher or lower state of existence. The goal is to break free from this cycle by achieving enlightenment.

4. Reincarnation

Reincarnation is the belief that after death, the soul is reborn into a new body. It is closely related to the concept of samsara and is based on the idea that our actions in this life will determine our future lives.

5. *"Moksha"*

"Moksha" is the goal of Hinduism – liberation from the cycle of birth, death, and rebirth. It is attained when one achieves enlightenment and breaks free from the cycle of samsara.

6. "*Karma Yoga*"

"*Karma yoga*" is the path of selfless action and service. It is based on the idea that by performing actions without any attachment to the outcome, one can accumulate good "*Karma*" and eventually reach enlightenment.

7. Karmic Debt

Karmic debt refers to the negative consequences of our past actions that we must pay in this life or future lives. It is believed that our actions in this life will determine our karmic debt and how we will be reborn in the next life.

8. *"Sanchita Karma"*

"Sanchita Karma" refers to the sum of all our past actions from previous lives that are yet to be experienced. It is believed that this accumulated *"Karma"* will determine our future lives and experiences.

9. *"Prarabdha Karma"*

"Prarabdha Karma" refers to the portion of our *"Sanchita Karma"* that has ripened and is ready to be experienced in this lifetime. It is the *"Karma"* that has brought us into this life and determines the events and circumstances we will face.

10. "*Agami Karma*"

"*Agami Karma*" refers to the new *"Karma"* we create in this lifetime through our actions, thoughts, and intentions. It adds to our *"Sanchita Karma"* and will determine our future lives and experiences.

11. "*Akarma*"

"*Akarma*" refers to non-action or inaction. It is believed that by not acting, one can avoid accumulating negative *"Karma"*. However, it is important to note that *"Akarma"* should not be confused with laziness or lack of responsibility.

12. "*Karma phala*"

"*Karma phala*" refers to the fruits or the results of our actions. It is believed that every action, whether good or bad, will have a corresponding outcome or consequence.

13. "*Kriyamana Karma*"

"*Kriyamana Karma*" refers to the *"Karma"* we create in this present moment. It is based on the idea that every thought, intention, and action has a consequence, and we are responsible for our present and future experiences.

14. "*Dridha Karma*"

Dridha "Karma" refers to fixed or firm *"Karma"* that cannot be changed or altered. It is the result of our past actions and is believed to be inevitable.

15. "*Adridha Karma*"

"Adridha Karma" refers to the *"Karma"* that can be changed or altered through our present actions. It is based on the belief that we have the power to change our destiny through our choices and actions.

16. *Pancha Mahayajnas*

Pancha Mahayajnas, also known as the *five great sacrifices*, are daily rituals performed by Hindus to fulfil their duties and responsibilities towards society, nature, ancestors, gods, and self. These sacrifices are believed to generate good *"Karma"* and balance out any negative *"Karma"*.

17. Law of Attraction

The law of attraction is a belief that like attracts like – positive thoughts attract positive experiences, while negative thoughts attract negative experiences. It is closely related to the concept of *"Karma"* as it emphasizes the power of our thoughts and intentions in creating our reality.

18. *"Karmic"* Balance

Karmic balance refers to the idea that every action has an equal and opposite reaction. It is based on the belief that we must always strive for balance in our actions and intentions to avoid accumulating negative *"Karma"*.

19. *"Karma"* Cleansing

"Karma" cleansing refers to the process of purifying one's accumulated negative *"Karma"* through acts of service, meditation, and spiritual practices. It is believed that by cleansing our *"Karma"*, we can improve our present and future lives.

20. *Bhagavad Gita*

The *Bhagavad Gita* is one of the most-revered Hindu scriptures that contains teachings on *dharma,* "Karma", *and moksha.* It is one of the most important texts on Hindu philosophy and is often used as a guide for living a righteous life.

In conclusion, *"Karma"* is a complex and multi-faceted concept that has different interpretations and beliefs attached to it. This comprehensive glossary of *"Karma"*-related terms aims to provide a better understanding of this concept and its various aspects. Whether you believe in *"Karma"* or not, it is undeniable that our actions have consequences, and by understanding the concept of *"Karma",* we can strive to live a more conscious and intentional life. As the saying goes, *"What goes around comes around,"* so let us strive to create positive ripples in the world through our thoughts, words, and actions.

@@@@

CHAPTER 23

RECOMMENDED READING AND RESOURCES

1. *Bhagavad Gita*

The *Bhagavad Gita* is a sacred Hindu text that discusses the concept of *"Karma"* in detail. It is a dialogue between the *Lord Krishna* and the great warrior *Arjuna*, who faced a moral dilemma on the battlefield of *Kurukshetra*. Krishna explains to *Arjuna* that it is his duty to fight and fulfil his *dharma* (life *purpose*) regardless of the outcome. This emphasizes the idea that our actions, not the results, are what truly matter in the eyes of *"Karma"*.

2. *The Tibetan Book of the Dead*

Also known as the *Bardo Thodol*, this Tibetan Buddhist text explores the concept of *"Karma"* in relation to death and rebirth. It explains how our actions in this life will determine our experiences in the intermediate state between death and rebirth. This book offers a unique perspective on *"Karma"* and its role in the cycle of life and death.

3. *The Art of Happiness* by Dalai Lama

This book by the 14th *Dalai Lama* explores how we can cultivate happiness in our lives through compassion, forgiveness, and taking responsibility for our actions. It also discusses how understanding the concept of *"Karma"* can help us lead a more fulfilling and purposeful life.

4. *"Karma": What It Is, What It Isn't, Why It Matters"* by *Traleg Kyabgon*

Written by a Tibetan Buddhist master, this book offers a comprehensive understanding of the concept of *"Karma"*. It explores its origins, different interpretations, and how it applies to our daily lives. It also discusses how we can use the concept of *"Karma"* to create positive change in our lives and in the world.

5. *"Karma" & Reincarnation: The Key to Spiritual Evolution and Enlightenment* "by *Torkom Saraydarian*

This book delves into the deeper meaning of *"Karma"* and how it relates to our spiritual evolution. It discusses how we can use our understanding of *"Karma"* to break free from negative patterns and reach higher levels of consciousness.

Recommended Resources on *"Karma"*

1. Podcast: *The "Karma" Chronicles*

Hosted by spiritual teacher *Deepa Manda*, this podcast explores the concept of *"Karma"* through discussions with experts, personal stories, and practical advice on how to incorporate the principles of *"Karma"* into our daily lives.

2. YouTube Channel: *Eckhart Tolle*

Eckhart Tolle, a spiritual teacher and author, has a vast collection of videos on YouTube exploring various spiritual concepts including *"Karma"*. His talks on *"Karma"* offer a unique perspective that helps us understand how we can break free from negative patterns and create a better future for ourselves.

3. Online Course: *The Science of "Karma"* **by The Great Courses**

This online course delves into the scientific and philosophical aspects of *"Karma"*, exploring its origins, principles, and how it has been interpreted throughout history. It also offers practical tips on how to use the concept of *"Karma"* to enhance our well-being and create a more harmonious world.

In conclusion, the concept of "Karma" is a complex and profound belief that has shaped the way many people view the world and their actions. Whether you are interested in exploring it from a philosophical, religious, or scientific perspective, there are many resources available to help you gain a deeper understanding of this concept. We hope this recommended reading and resources on *"Karma"* will guide you on your journey towards understanding this fascinating belief system. Remember, what we put out into the world will eventually come back to us in some form or another, so let us strive to create good *"Karma"* through our actions, thoughts, and intentions.

@@@@

CHAPTER 24

REFLECTION QUESTIONS AND EXERCISES: "THE *KARMA* PUZZLE"

"*The Karma Puzzle: Understanding the Law of Cosmic Justice*" offers profound insights into karma's intricacies. To deepen understanding and integration, this article provides comprehensive reflection questions and exercises.

Part 1: Understanding "Karma"

1. Define "*Karma*" in your own words.

2. How does "*Karma*" influence daily decisions?

3. Reflect on personal experiences where "*Karma*" played a significant role.

4. What are common misconceptions about "*Karma*"?

5. How does "*Karma*" relate to personal responsibility?

Exercises:

1. **Journaling:** Record daily actions, thoughts, and intentions. Analyse patterns.

2. **Meditation:** Contemplate "*Karma*'s universal principles.

3. **Research:** Study "*Karma*" in various spiritual traditions.

Part 2: Intention and Action

1. What drives your intentions: desires, values, or habits?

2. How do actions align with values and goals?

3. Recall situations where intention and action clashed.

4. What role does mindfulness play in intentional action?

5. How can self-awareness improve decision-making?

Exercises:

1. **Intention-setting:**

Clarify goals, align with values.

2. **Mindfulness practice:**

Observe thoughts, emotions driving actions.

3. **Self-reflection:**

Identify areas for personal growth.

Part 3: Cause and Effect

1. What causes have you set in motion?

2. How have past actions influenced current circumstances?

3. Consider challenging situations: What "*Karma*" may be at play?

4. What lessons can be learned from past experiences?

5. How can awareness of cause-and-effect guide decision-making?

Exercises:

1. **Causality mapping:**

Visualize cause-and-effect relationships.

2. **Self-reflection:**

Identify areas for personal growth.

3. **Journaling**:

Track progress, insights.

Part 4: Personal Responsibility

1. Where do you take responsibility in life?

2. How do you hold yourself accountable?

3. Reflect on blaming others or circumstances.

4. What role does self-compassion play in personal responsibility?

5. How can self-awareness enhance accountability?

Exercises:

1. **Accountability partner:**

Share goals, progress.

2. **Self-inquiry:**

Examine motivations, choices.

3. **Mindfulness:**

Observe self-criticism.

Part 5: Forgiveness and Release

1. What burdens do you carry?

2. How can you forgive yourself and others?

3. Recall situations where forgiveness freed you.

4. What role does self-forgiveness play in personal growth?

5. How can letting go of attachment promote freedom?

Exercises:

1. **Forgiveness letter:** Write, release emotions.

2. **Letting-go ritual**: Symbolize release.

3. **Meditation:** Focus on self-compassion.

Part 6: Spiritual Growth

1. How does "*Karma*" impact spiritual evolution?

2. What spiritual practices enhance "*Karma*"?

3. Reflect on personal growth through "*Karma*".

4. What role does mindfulness play in spiritual growth?

5. How can self-awareness facilitate spiritual evolution?

Exercises:

1. **Meditation:** Focus on spiritual growth.

2. **Journaling:** Track progress, insights.

3. **Self-reflection:** Identify areas for spiritual exploration.

Conclusion

Introspection, self-awareness, and intentional action are required to properly comprehend the concept of "*Karma*" *and* live a life of happiness and bliss. *These reflection questions and exercises empower you to:*

1. Clarify "*Karma*'s role in life.

2. Align intentions and actions.

3. Take personal responsibility.

4. Cultivate forgiveness and release.

5. Foster spiritual growth

By exploring these questions and exercises, deepen your understanding of "*Karma*" and unlock the "*Karma*" puzzle.

Additional Resources:

1. "The ***Bhagavad Gita***"

2. "**The Power of Now**" by *Eckhart Tolle*

3. "**The Art of Happiness**" by *Dalai Lama*

4. Online courses: *Karma, mindfulness, spiritual growth*

5. Spiritual communities: *Local centres, online forums*

@@@@

Also by Dr.A.K.Saxena, Ph.D.

Handbook for Introverted Leaders: Strategies for Success
No Longer a Yes Man
Fasting, Feasting and Spirituality
The "Karma" Puzzle
Open Secrets